Magic Guidebooks

Disneyland®

2018

Secrets, Money-Saving Tips, Hidden Mickeys,
Fast Pass Hacks and Everything Else
You Need to Know in a Single Guide!

Magic Guidebooks

Disneyland 2018

Priceless Information and reviews all in one guide!

Coverage of Disneyland, Disney California Adventure, Downtown Disney, and Beyond!

Hacks for FastPass, MaxPass and Tips to Skip the Lines!

Money-Saving Tips for Tickets, Hotels, Travel, and More!

Ride and Restaurant Reviews & Recommendations!

Bonus! Guide to Universal Studios Hollywood!

Plus! Coverage for Los Angeles Attractions, San Diego Zoo, and LEGOLAND!

Table of Contents

Get Updated!
Sign up for our Free E-Mail List:

www.magicguidebooks.com/signup

Follow Us

Instagram
@magicguides

About This Guide

When writing and designing this book, we had *you* in mind. Maybe you're a first-time visitor to the Disneyland Resort or perhaps, you've frequented for many years. Wherever you come from and whatever your experience, we wanted to provide a complete guide from start to finish, while giving a critique of the attractions and restaurants in the resort. In fact, the entire purpose of this guide is to give real advice covering the many attractions, restaurants, and hotels from the Disneyland Resort and beyond.

Who are we? Well, we're theme park enthusiasts who spend a lot of time gathering first-hand knowledge and experiences from all around the world. In fact, we've visited every Disney Resort, including the new Shanghai Disneyland, because we love them so much. In other words, advice in this guide is crafted from trial and error–and we're passing the fruits of our hard work onto you!

The Disneyland Resort is a constantly changing place. From exciting themed dining to limited-time thrilling attractions, sometimes we could never imagine what might be coming next! Since experiences come and go, we also invite you to subscribe to our free e-mail list for up-to-date travel information. Visit our website and sign up today **www.magicguidebooks.com**

Keep in mind that this guide is an "unofficial edition", meaning that we are in no way affiliated with the Walt Disney Company®, the Disneyland Resort®, the Walt Disney World® Resort, and nor have we ever been. We are simply fans of the Disneyland Resort® who are giving an honest opinion on what it has to offer.

CHAPTER ONE

INTRODUCTION TO THE DISNEYLAND RESORT

"The Happiest Place on Earth!"

The Disneyland Resort in California is home to virtually countless attractions, thrilling and classic rides, and gourmet food perfect for people of all ages. With two breathtaking theme parks (Disneyland and Disney California Adventure), three stylish hotels, and a dazzling Downtown Disney for shopping and restaurants, it's no wonder that millions of people flock to Disneyland from all over the world!

So, why is it "The Happiest Place on Earth"? The truth is, no matter our age, Disneyland brings us back to feeling like a kid again in a place that allows us to be! From world-class rides, stunning fireworks, delicious food, themed lands designed for everyone, and bars for adults–the Disneyland Resort has it all! In short, whether you like thrilling rides like *Indiana Jones* and *Guardians of the Galaxy - Mission Breakout* or seeing a spectacular show like *World of Color* or *Paint the Night*, you will be floored by the magic at Disneyland!

So, Why Do I Need a Book?

While you can visit to the Disneyland Resort any time and attempt to experience on your own, having invaluable tips from insiders will save you time, hassle, and money. This guide will save you time waiting in lines, money, and give you the best options to fit your mood. We visit the Disneyland Resort more times in a year than we can count and we know all the ins and outs of the parks.

Whether you are looking to ride all of the thrilling attractions in one day, two days, or don't like rides at all, this book will be your guide. Even if you are visiting with kids, other adults, or by yourself, we've got you covered! Packed with insider secrets–we call them "Magic Tips"–for where to get the best food, little-known experiences, hidden adventures, and more, this book will be your ultimate guide to the Disneyland Resort!

I've Been to Walt Disney World —Should I Still Visit Disneyland?

As native Southern Californians, Disneyland has a special place in our hearts. Truthfully, we believe that there is a magic in the Disneyland Resort that doesn't exist at any other Disney theme park. While we *love* Disney World, Walt Disney created Disneyland–he unfortunately passed before Walt Disney World was completed–and the magic residing in the Disneyland Park comes from Walt himself.

The Cast Members (Disney employees) are always helpful and friendly and the parks are impeccably clean! Sure, many of the rides are similarly themed both Resorts, like *Pirates of the Caribbean* and *Big Thunder Mountain Railroad* (though you'll notice plenty of differences in these rides), but the Disneyland Resort exists with more detail in the parks that create a magic unlike anywhere else.

We will add that the Disney World castle is much larger (over 100 feet taller than the Sleeping Beauty Castle in California), and many Disney World fanatics notice this first. However, Disneyland and Disney California Adventure have unique attractions like the Matterhorn Bobsleds, Cars Land, Indiana Jones Adventure, the seasonal Haunted Mansion Holiday starring the characters from Tim Burton's *The Nightmare Before Christmas*, to name a few. Even better, Disneyland and Disney California Adventure are located right across from one another, so you won't have to haul on busses from park to park like at Walt Disney World.

How Many Days Should I Book?

Between the parks–Disneyland and Disney California Adventure–and Downtown Disney, there appear to be countless attractions to visit. We'd recommend anywhere from 2-4 days to satisfy a trip. If you want to stay longer, there is plenty to do! In this guide, we will show you how to experience Disneyland and California Adventure in one day, two days, three days, a week or more based on our suggestions, pre-planned ride list, and reviews of the Resort's attractions, and delicious dining.

CHAPTER TWO

DISNEYLAND PHRASES AND RESOURCES

Introduction

If you are new to the Disney theme parks or just haven't been in some time, you'll instantly notice a new lingo at the parks. Whether you're talking to a fellow guest, Cast Member, or reading signs by rides, it helps to know the terms first.

Secondly, we have our own phrases that we use frequently throughout this book. Most of these phrases are fairly intuitive, but so that we are all on the same page, we invite you to familiarize yourself with the section to help with reading this guide.

Phrases and Words for Disneyland

The Disneyland Resort - The area that encompasses both theme parks (Disneyland and Disney California Adventure), Downtown Disney, the 3 hotels, and the parking lots.

Cast Member - A term for all Disney employees. We find that the Disneyland Resort Cast Members are the friendliest of them all!

Park Hopper - A ticket that allows you to visit both Disneyland and Disney California Adventure as many times as you'd like during that day.

"Dark Ride" - An indoor ride where the vehicle is guided along a track. Typically, these are family-friendly rides like "it's a small world" and "They also have air conditioning to escape the heat on hot days!

FastPass - An easy and free way to cut the lines! FastPass kiosks are set up throughout Disneyland and Disney California Adventure near most popular attractions. Simply insert your park ticket and a FastPass reminder will be distributed to you for the corresponding ride. You still may need your ticket to scan before getting on the ride.

MaxPass - An optional feature to use with FastPass and PhotoPass. For $10 a day (introductory price) you can get unlimited downloads of Disney PhotoPass and reserve your FastPass reservation from the Disneyland mobile application!

Single Rider Line - A fast way to get on the rides as long as you don't mind traveling by yourself.
Note: We've included a complete list of rides with FastPass and Single Rider Lines in Chapter Sixteen on page 234.

Passholders - Those who purchased Annual Passes.

3D - The use of 3D glasses during the ride or attraction.

4D - The use of 3D glasses with added effects like splashing water and rumbling seats.

Closed for Refurbishment - No one likes seeing this sign as it means that the ride is closed for restoration. Some refurbishments can last a couple of days, while others have lasted years. Refurbishment scheduling occurs most in the off-season months like January through March.

The Disneyland Resort plans their refurbishments carefully and will post these on the entertainment schedule:
https://disneyland.disney.go.com/calendars/day

Phrases and Words for this Guide Book

⋆ **Magic Tips** ⋆ - These are special tips and secrets from our personal experience after visiting the Disneyland Resort several times a year.

Magic Tips are designed to...

- Save time waiting in lines
- Get the best viewing areas for shows and parades
- Save money booking
- And *a lot* more! We love Disneyland and want to share our resort and theme park secrets with you!

Top Choice! - Found on our Top 8 List of most-recommended restaurants and eateries.

Ride Levels

Thrill Riders - Those looking for themed rollercoasters, drop rides, and other thrill will enjoy these picks

Everyone - Perfect for anyone of all ages, even many Thrill Riders enjoy these attractions

Family - Suited for anyone of all ages, both kids and adults. However, these rides may not interest Thrill Riders

Kids - Designed for kids ages 6-10

Young Kids - Designed for young kids 2-5

Restaurant Types

Table service - Restaurants with a waiter. It is suggested you that you tip based on the service you receive.

Fast Service - Meals that you can order and seat right away.

Cafeteria Style - Serve yourself from a selection of items and pay before you eat. These spaces often have ample bench seating.

"On-The-Go" Meal - This may be self-explanatory, but some of the meals in Disney are packed and ready to go. These are often meals you eat while watching a show in preferred seating.

Restaurant Pricing:
$ - Under $10 (typically snack carts)
$$ - $10 - $15 (typically Fast Service Restaurants)
$$$ - $15 - $25 (more expensive Fast Service Restaurants)
$$$$ - $25 or more (premium dining like the Blue Bayou and Carthay Circle)

Contact Information

Disneyland.com
Visit for booking and reservations.

Hotel Reservations (714) 781-6425
https://disneyland.disney.go.com/hotels

Disney Dining (714) 781-DINE
Book your restaurant reservations in advance.
https://disneyland.disney.go.com/dining

Tickets (714) 781-4565
Book your tickets in advance
https://disneyland.disney.go.com/tickets

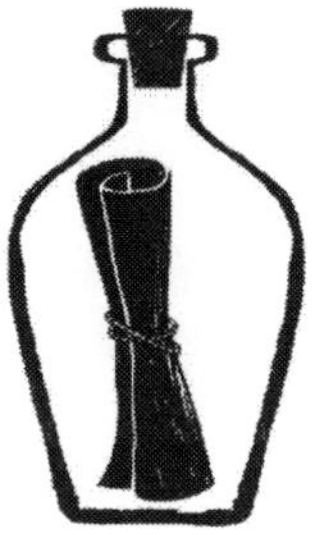

Other Booking Websites with Discounts

DisneyRewards.com - If you have a Disney Visa® Card, earn points and claim special rewards.

Orbitz.com/deals - For special promotions (look for codes up to 15% Off hotels).

Bookit.com/coupon-codes - Search here for discounts on flights, hotels, and ticket bundles.

Amextravel.com - If you have an American Express Card, this can save you, plus earn more rewards.

Costcotravel.com - If you have a Costco Membership, you might save big on vacation packages and tickets.

CHAPTER THREE

WHY VISIT DISNEYLAND IN 2018?

Introduction

In the year before the highly anticipated Star Wars-themed land is set to open at Disneyland, 2018 might be one of the last great years to take advantage of shorter wait times in less-crowded parks. Several new attractions from 2017 and 2018 will also make this a year to remember!

Beat the Crowds

Beat the Crowds Before Star Wars: Galaxy's Edge

Disneyland

Star Wars is coming to the Disneyland Resort in the most exciting way! Several acres of the Disneyland theme park have gone under construction to make way for likely the most-anticipated themed land since the Wizarding World of Harry Potter at Universal Studios. Star Wars: Galaxy's Edge isn't set to open until Summer 2019. However, we don't recommend waiting until then as the park will likely be packed with eager guests. Galaxy's Edge will feature two new rides including a Millennium Falcon flight simulator and a ride where you will escape the grasp of the evil First Order! Along with life-like costumed characters and realistic animatronics, this Star Wars-themed land will be a reason to return after your visit in 2018!

New Attractions

Pixar Pier

Disney California Adventure

Join your favorite Pixar characters from "Toy Story", "Inside Out", "The Incredibles" and more in this newly re-themed land! Pixar Pier will take over the previous Paradise Pier, re-imagining the classic California Screamin' rollercoaster and even adding new attractions! We also expect a new ride or two that have yet to be announced. Pixar Pier is set to open in Summer 2018, just in time for you to enjoy the excitement!

Guardians of the Galaxy - Mission: Breakout

Disney California Adventure

The popular Twilight Zone Tower of Terror has been transformed into Disneyland's first Marvel-themed ride! You'll plummet over a dozen stories as you and the Guardians attempt to escape The Collector's evil grasp! Mission: Breakout opened Spring 2017, so 2018 will be the best time to avoid the long lines from last year!

Returning Attractions

Paint the Night

Disney California Adventure

The dazzling and popular nighttime parade will return with new floats and will switch to California Adventure in 2018!

CHAPTER FOUR

PLANNING YOUR DISNEYLAND RESORT VACATION

When to Visit the Disneyland Resort

Wanting to go to Disneyland is easy - planning it can be a whole other animal! The good news is, we're here to help. We've been to the Disneyland Resort more than we can count and we've picked up hundreds of useful tips for you. In this part of the guide, we will walk you through the choices of travel and our recommendations for saving time and money.

Choosing a time for your vacation may not be entirely up to you. It could depend on allowed vacation from work, your travel schedule, or your children's vacation days from school. Whether you have flexible travel days or not, we have laid out a month-by-month breakdown of what to expect when you visit the Disneyland Resort. We also give you tips on how to avoid the long lines and more to save you time and make your stay a very enjoyable one!

Most Recommended Travel Months

1. **September** - Summer continues throughout September in Southern California. Expect hot days and far less crowds than in June, July, and August. Halloween begins mid-September!

2. **October** - Disneyland and Disney California Adventure come alive during Halloween with typically perfect weather. Decorations, desserts, special rides, and Mickey's Halloween Party await you!

3. **February** - The Disneyland Resort typically has fewer crowds at this time, though weekends can be busy.

Least Recommended Travel Months

1. **July** - Massive crowds from all over the world flood Disneyland. Expect higher ticket prices, long lines, and very hot weather.

2. **December** - While park guests are treated to the holiday decorations, treats, and special rides, the crowds are some of the most massive. If you must go in December, we recommend the first week.

3. **August** - Similar to July with the crowds, but August thins out in the last week when the kids get back to school. Keep in mind that the weather is blazing hot in Southern California at that time. The last two weeks of August can be ideal times to visit once school is in session.

Note: *Are you planning to be at the resort during one of our least recommended months? Don't worry! This guide will help you avoid those long lines. Be sure to follow one of our pre-planned attraction lists - we use them ourselves and they can save you hours of time waiting in lines–or avoid them altogether. Tips for beating the crowds are at the end of this chapter.*

Day Breakdown

Sunday - Weekend crowds, but far less than Saturday.

Monday - Often these can be just as crowded as Sundays because people take off extra days to avoid weekend traffic. On Monday holidays, expect very larger crowds.

Tuesday - Typically has the fewest crowds

Wednesday - Typically has second fewest crowds

Thursday - Third most recommended day for fewest crowds

Friday - Less busy in the morning, but busiest in the evening after school is out for the Annual Passholders.

Saturday - The busiest day at the resort.

Holidays - It's best to avoid the busy holidays and three day weekends (Friday through Tuesday) as they get very busy.

Note: *These days always depend on the month, but this is a general idea of how to avoid the largest crowds.*

Best Days to Visit

• The 1st or 2nd weeks in February (especially Tuesdays and Wednesdays)
• The last week in January (unless it's near the Martin Luther King, Jr. Day Holiday on the 3rd Monday of January)
• 2nd week of September (but not around Labor Day)

Most Crowded Days

1. Christmas Day (and week)
2. New Year's Eve/Day
3. Thanksgiving week
4. Memorial Day weekend
5. Fourth of July
6. Labor Day weekend
7. Veterans Day

★ **Magic Tip** ★

Disneyland's new tier pricing will be higher (Peak pricing) on more crowded days and lower (Value pricing) on less crowded days.

Visit the ticketing website **disneyland.disney.go.com/tickets** for Value, Regular, and Peak pricing.

Month Breakdown

January

Overview: January is busy in the first two weeks, and generally less busy after that. The first week will be crowded from and filled with holiday rides, treats, music, and decorations lighting the resort.

Weather: mid-60°F (15°C) during the day and chilly at night

Least Crowded Days: last week in January

Most Crowded: first two weeks (especially around New Years) and Martin Luther King Jr. Weekend (Friday - Tuesday)

Holiday Rides and Attractions:

1. Haunted Mansion Holiday (Tim Burton's *The Nightmare Before Christmas*)
2. "it's a small world" Holiday
3. Jingle Cruise (Jungle Cruise Holiday)
4. World of Color - Winter Dreams
5. Meet Santa Claus at Elias & Co.

★ **Magic Tips** ★
Holiday rides typically continue through the first week of January.
Disneyland and Disney California Adventure may have ride closures for refurbishments after the holiday decorations come down.

February

Overview: Possibly the least crowded month to visit the Disneyland Resort. Like January, the weather is cooler, and some of the rides may be in refurbishment.
Weather: Low-70°F (21°C) during the day and chilly at night. However, February has been known to have heatwaves, bring the weather above 90°F (32°C).
Least Crowded Days: Any week except near President's Day Weekend (Friday - Tuesday)
Most Crowded: President's Day Weekend (Friday - Tuesday)
Lunar New Year: Celebrate the year of the Dog at California Adventure. Watch a spectacular nighttime show at World of Color on Paradise Pier and meet characters like Mulan and Mushu!
For dates, visit: https://disneyland.disney.go.com/events-tours/lunar-new-year/

★ **Magic Tip** ★ Disneyland and Disney California Adventure may have more ride closures for refurbishments in February than other months.

Springtime Discounts

The Disneyland Resort often has a discounted ticket offer for Southern Californians from March through May. Also, hotels may be on discount, usually around 25%. Visit Disneyland.com for updates on these.

Food and Wine Festival

Mid-March to mid-April

Every spring, California Adventure lines the street between Buena Vista and Paradise Pier with delicious seasonal food and adult beverages. You can sip and savor at several booths from creamy mac n cheese to California-grown wines. The menu changes from year to year, and we highly recommend tasting your way through the most delicious-sounding treats.

★ **Magic Tip** ★

Disney offers a "pass" to sample the different booths, but the pricing of this pass doesn't save you any money. While this could change in 2018, we still recommend looking at the selections *a la cart* before purchasing this pass.

March

Overview: March's popularity has increased recently as spring breaks spread throughout the month. If you visit in March, be sure to do so during the week, Tuesday through Thursday.
Weather: mid-70°F (21°C) during the day and chilly at night. However, March has been known to have occasional heatwaves, bring the weather above 90°F (32°C).
Least Crowded Days: the first Tuesday, Wednesday, and Thursday of March
Most Crowded: Last two weeks of the month.
Deals:

- Disneyland Resort hotels will often have discounted pricing during this time.
- Southern Californians can enjoy discounts on multi-day tickets.

★ **Magic Tip** ★
Like February, Disneyland and Disney California Adventure may have some ride closures for refurbishments.

April

Overview: With spring breaks continuing through April, the end of the month tends to be the least crowded.
Weather: Mid-70°F (21°C) during the day and chilly at night.
Least Crowded Days: The last two weeks of the month.
Most Crowded: First two weeks of the month.

Special Days:

Bats Day - (April 29 - May 1st) - Goths (typically dressed in black) from far and wide venture to the park for this weekend. For more information, visit **www.BatsDay.net**

Note: *April is also subject to ride refurbishments*

May

Overview: Spring in Disneyland is beautiful with the sun and toward the end of the month, it will already feel like Summer.
Weather: Mid-70°F (21°C) during the day and sometimes chilly at night.
Least Crowded Days: The first two weeks of the month.
Most crowded: Memorial Day weekend (Friday - Tuesday).

Special Days:

Bats Day - (April 29 - May 1st) - See April for details.
Dapper Day - Spring (May 1st) - See guests dressed in their "Sunday Best" on this unofficial, yet widely celebrated day. If you are interested in participating, visit: **DapperDay.com** for more details. This semi-annual day also occurs in November.

★ **Magic Tip** ★
May is also subject to ride refurbishments, but they usually wrap up before Memorial Day.

Deals:

- Disneyland Resort hotels will often have discounted pricing during this time.
- Southern Californians can enjoy discounts on multi-day tickets.

June

Overview: The warm June weather perfectly suits the Disneyland Resort.
Weather: Mid-80°F (27°C) during the day. Typically keeps warm at night.
Least crowded days: Tuesday, Wednesdays, and Thursdays and the first week of the month.
Most crowded: The last week of the month.

Deals: Disneyland Resort hotels will often have discounted pricing during this time.

★ **Magic Tip** ★
June is a bit of an unpredictable crowd month as school are closed and summer vacations begin.

July

Overview: The weather heats up (sometimes unbearably so) and crowds from all over the world venture into the Disneyland Resort during July.
Weather: High-80°F (27°C) during the day. Typically keeps warm at night.
Least Crowded Days: Tuesday, Wednesdays, and Thursdays (unless one is July 4th)
Most Crowded: July 4th

Disney's Celebrate America!
Catch a stunning fireworks spectacular on and around July 4, 2018! See American flag projections on the castle, red, white, and blue fireworks, and patriotic music playing throughout the Disneyland park!

Note: *If you are planning to visit in July, we highly recommend our tips for beating the crowds at the end of this chapter.*

August

Overview: The weather continues to heat up even more in August as crowds continue to pour in until school begins.
Weather: Mid-90°F (32°C) during the day. Typically keeps very warm at night.
Least Crowded Days: Tuesday, Wednesdays, and Thursdays and the last two weeks of the month.
Most Crowded: The first 2 weeks of the month.

September

Overview: More hot weather typically all month long with Halloween rides and treats beginning mid-September.
Weather: High-90°F (32°C) during the day. Typically keeps very warm at night.
Least Crowded Days: Tuesday, Wednesdays, Thursdays, and Fridays (except for Mickey's Halloween Party nights)
Most Crowded: Labor Day weekend.

Note: See October for Disneyland Halloween details

October

Overview: October is a favorite time of ours at the Disneyland Resort! The weather cools down as the Halloween party kicks into full gear at both parks!
Weather: Low-80°F (27°C) during the day, cools at night.
Least Crowded Days: Tuesday, Wednesdays, and Thursdays
Most Crowded: Halloween and Mickey's Halloween Party nights on select dates.

Halloween at the Disneyland Resort

Mickey's Halloween Party begins! A perfect time to dress in costume (all ages) and get some treats. This is a special event and is not included with a standard ticket. See Disneyland.com for dates and to purchase (usually announced in the Summer)

Halloween Holiday Rides and Attractions

- Haunted Mansion Holiday (Disneyland) - Jack Skellington and his friends from Tim Burton's *The Nightmare Before Christmas* take over the Haunted Mansion. The attraction features new animatronics, special effects, and music through the first week of January.

- Space Mountain: Ghost Galaxy (Disneyland) - a terrifying ghost follows you throughout the ride!
- Guardians of the Galaxy – Monsters After Dark (California Adventure) - help save Groot from rampaging alien monsters that have taken over The Collector's Fortress!
- Cars Land Haul-O-Ween Celebration (California Adventure) - Cars Land completely decorated for the spooky holiday. Luigi's Rollickin' Roadsters and Mater's Junkyard Jamboree get Halloween Makeovers with new music and fun for the entire family.
- Frightfully Fun Parade (Disneyland) - a ghastly parade inspired by Disney Villains Jack Skellington!
- See massive Mickey-shaped pumpkins, try delicious treats, and see your favorite characters dressed in their Halloween costumes!
- Oogie Boogie takes over California Adventure with frightful flying bats and other mischief down Buena Vista Street and throughout Cars Land! The Headless Horseman statue also makes an appearance!

Halloween Treat Highlights

- Pumpkin Flan - Rancho del Zocalo Restaurante (Frontierland)
- Bat Mickey Cookie - Market House (Main Street)
- Pumpkin Twist - Maurice's Treats (Fantasyland)
- Pumpkin Muffin, Pumpkin Spice Latte, and Pumpkin Cheesecake - Jolly Holiday Bakery Café (Main Street)
- Halloween Premium Cone - Gibson Girl Ice Cream Parlor (Main Street)

Special Days: Gay Days (October 5-7th) - an unofficial event for LGBT families and singles to wear red in the parks. Visit www.gaydaysanaheim.com for more information

★ **Magic Tip** ★
Mickey's Halloween Party can be packed! To avoid some of these crazy times, book your tickets during the first half of the event dates.

November

Overview: The holidays begin mid-November at the Disneyland Resort. Expect larger crowds beginning Veterans Day and forward. *See for December for Disneyland Holiday details.*
Weather: Mid-70°F (21°C) during the day, cools at night to 50°F (10°C).
Least Crowded Days: The first week of the month.
Most Crowded: Veteran's Day and Thanksgiving week.

Special Days:

Dapper Day - Autumn (November 6th) - see guests dressed in their "Sunday Best" on this unofficial, yet widely celebrated day (also occurs in May). If you are interested in participating, visit: DapperDay.com for more details.

December

Overview: The holidays are in full gear at the Disneyland Resort. See decorations all around with special treats, fun holiday-themed rides, and a chance to meet Santa Claus!
Weather: Low-60°F (15°C) during the day, can cool at night to mid-40°F (5°C).

Least Crowded Days: The first week of the month.
Most Crowded: The last two weeks, especially Christmas Day and New Year's Eve.

Holidays at the Disneyland Resort:

See the glimmering Christmas lights decorating the Disneyland Resort! From magnificent Christmas trees to endless strings of lights and ornaments, you'll be in awe of the resort's holiday transformation!

Holiday Rides and Attractions:

- Haunted Mansion Holiday - Jack Skellington and his friends from Tim Burton's *The Nightmare Before Christmas* continue their takeover of the Haunted Mansion. The attraction features new animatronics, special effects, and music through the first week of January.
- "Jingle Cruise" - Jungle Cruise gets a Christmas layover with holiday humor and decor around the riverboat ride.
- "it's a small world" holiday - See the magnificent lights that illuminate this classic attraction on the outside. Inside, see the wondrous holidays celebrated all around the world.
- A Christmas Fantasy Parade (Disneyland) - Mickey, Santa, Disney Princesses celebrate Christmas aboard stunning floats
- World of Color: Winter Dreams (Disney California Adventure) - light up the night with a spectacular water show perfectly designed for the holiday season. Watch your favorite Disney characters come to life and celebrate the joy of the season.

- Meet Santa Claus in Critter Country (Disneyland) or Elias & Co. (Disney California Adventure) and meet Mickey and his friends in their holiday clothing. Don't forget to say hi to Jack Skellington and Sally near Haunted Mansion!

Holiday Treat Highlights:

- Praline Cheese Cake - French Market Restaurant (New Orleans Square)
- Holiday Crispy (rice crispy) - Bengal Barbecue (Frontierland) and Refreshment Corner (Main Street, U.S.A.)
- Holiday Peppermint Mocha - Café Orleans and Blue Bayou Restaurant (New Orleans Square)
- Peppermint Ice Cream (candy cane cones also available) - Gibson Girl Ice Cream Parlor (Main Street, U.S.A.)
- Gingerbread Man Cookie - Golden Horseshoe (Frontierland)
- Yule Logs (Pumpkin and Chocolate Coffee) - Plaza Inn Restaurant (Main Street, U.S.A.)
- Eggnog Latte - Royal Street Veranda (New Orleans Square)
- Holiday Brownie and Snowman Shortbread Cookie - Village Haus Restaurant (Fantasyland)

Tips for Beating the Crowds

—Even on the Busiest Days

1. **Be Early** - Get to the park at open before the crowds. You will thank us for this tip when you see how effective it is!

2. **Plan Your Day** - Follow one of our pre-set day plans (or make your own). We use these planners ourselves and it will save you hours of time waiting in lines (many times you'll miss the long lines altogether).

3. **Use FastPass** - As early as possible, get passes to the rides that you want to experience.

4. Avoid Typical Meal Times:

a. Lunch: Dine before 11.30am and after 2.30pm

b. Dinner: Dine before 5.00pm and after 7.30pm

5. **Book Dining Reservations** - Reservations can be made at Disneyland.com 60 days in advance.

6. **Move to Disney California Adventure** - Disneyland can have many larger crowds than Disney California Adventure, especially in the morning. If the crowds are too much at Disneyland, head to the opposite park and see what you can ride or see there.

7. **You Might Have to Wait** - Waiting in line isn't the end of the world. Sometimes we all have to do it for the best attractions. The trick is to wait the *shortest* amount of time for the *fewest* rides possible. You can avoid the longest lines by following our planned out ride lists.

8. **Use Extra Magic Hours** - If you are staying at a Disneyland Resort hotel you can sometimes enter one of the parks early. The calendar on Disneyland's website will list these special times. Guests with Extra Magic hours in the morning have access to a special line to cut the rest of the guests as well as early access to FastPasses!

9. **Avoid Extra Magic Hours** - If you are not staying at a resort hotel, you might want to avoid the park with Extra Magic Hours, as you won't be able to experience the attractions until the regular park hours begin. Also, Extra Magic Hours can attract huge amounts of guests, especially at Disneyland (California Adventure doesn't get the same amount of pull).

10. **Take a Break** - If you are feeling worn out, take a break at your hotel or visit Downtown Disney. The resort offers so many surprises that you might have blast drinking a cup of coffee while you listen to music near Starbucks rather than surrounded by a swarm of people. After you and your group have recharged, head back into the parks.

CHAPTER FIVE
BOOKING YOUR DISNEYLAND VACATION

Tips for Before You Book

Pre-book your Hotel - The further out you book your hotel, the less expensive it tends to be. Please refer to our Hotels Overview to read our hotel recommendations for your trip!

Fly into LAX (Los Angeles International) - If you are planning to fly, we recommend LAX because it tends to be the least expensive and easiest to travel from. LAX is located right next to highways that will take you to Disneyland.

Bundle - Sometimes purchasing a flight/hotel/car package from Disneyland.com or 3rd party travel site can save you some money. However, booking tickets and a hotel room together usually doesn't save your anything at all. To save on tickets, purchase multi-day park passes.

Know the Ticket Pricing Structure:

- Park tickets vary in pricing for each day
- Tickets are broken into 3 categories

  Value: $97 (typically Monday - Thursday)

  Regular: $110 (typically Friday - Sunday)

  Peak: $124 (holiday weeks, summer, spring break)
- Park Hoppers are an extra $50 - $60 for a single day
- You can save on both parks by booking consecutive days
- Visit: https://disneyland.disney.go.com/tickets for specific pricing for the dates you've chosen

Booking Discounts

There are many ways to save on booking your stay at the Disneyland Resort. Some are better than others depending on the offer. Here are our most recommended choices based on how much they can save you:

Bookit.com (877-742-9891)

highly recommended!

Perfect for flying/hotel packages with ticket options.

Pros of booking at Bookit.com

- Payment plans available with a down payment
- Big discounts on flights when you book a vacation package
- Disneyland Resort Hotels available (you'll still get all of the Resort hotel benefits including Extra Magic Hour)
- We tend to notice that Bookit.com has a different selection of available hotel rooms than other third party sites
- Lists Disneyland's "Good Neighbor Hotels" so you can see the closest hotels for what Disneyland recommends

- Bundle park tickets for slight discounts. Save on multiday park hopper tickets and to other parks including Universal Studios Hollywood
- Discounted car rental options and inexpensive travel insurance available

Cons

- When you just book a hotel without airfare, this website can sometimes be more expensive than other third parties
- Some of the better deals cannot be cancelled
- Often cancellation comes with a fee. Many other companies offer free cancellation without this fee

  Promo Code: www.bookit.com/coupon-codes

Disneyland.com (714-520-5060)

Tips

- Check the Disneyland.com website for discounts on hotels and more. Here you can book any of the three resort hotels, purchase tickets, and add features
- Spring Time (March - June) typically has the lowest fares.
- When Disneyland.com has sales, usually the third party websites will as well.

Benefits of booking at Disneyland.com

- Just put $200.00 down when you book for your entire package. The balance is typically due a 30 days before your trip begins
- A larger selection of rooms than offered by third party sites
- You can add flights, transportation, character dining, and tickets to other theme parks
- Disneyland.com often has flexible cancellation policies for full refunds, including park tickets

Cons

- The travel insurance is a lot pricier than most other sites
- You may save money booking with third party sites

Disneyland Military Discounts (714-520-7088)

The Disneyland Resort now offers discounted tickets for active and retired U.S. military. These discounts are found on military bases and include fantastic deals on 3 and 4-day tickets. Military will also save on Disney PhotoPass packages.

Additionally, the Disneyland Resort will sometimes make rooms available at a discount for military families. These can also be found at military outlets.

Other great 3rd Party Sites

Orbitz.com - *highly recommended!*

- Vacation packages available for Disneyland Hotels and other close resorts
- Promo codes: www.orbitz.com/deals (often 15% off)
- Earn Rewards when you sign up for their discount plan.

***Note**: often we find that booking separate hotels on Orbitz.com and a separate flight on Southwest.com are the least expensive options.*

Southwest.com

- Often the best deals on flights with 2 free checked bags
- Southwest offers open seating
- Tip: If you want to sit next to your friend or family member (especially if you have young children), we highly recommend purchasing the "Early Bird" for $15 each way
- Flight, hotel, and car packages available via SouthwestVacations.com

- Southwest does not charge fees for changing flights (see their website for details)

Priceline.com

Great hotel selections and vacation packages on an easy to use site. It's hard to find promotional codes for Priceline, but they have great prices.

Purchasing Park Tickets

We recommend saving money by booking tickets early (in case prices go up). The more tickets you purchase, the more you tend to save. Sometimes 3rd-party websites will save you a bit on booking multiday park hopper tickets.

Disneyland.com (714-520-5060)

- Get ticket bundles and more
- Comes with Magic Morning on certain days with a 3-Day ticket. Visit the park early in the morning up to an hour before the park opens
- Spring Time Multi-Day Discounts for Southern California Residents (March - May)
- Allows you to print tickets, have them mailed, or use your mobile device for eTickets
- When Disneyland.com has sales, usually the 3rd-party websites will as well
- Tickets are nonrefundable (if you bundle them with a hotel, they may be refundable)

Southern California CityPASS

A bundled ticket for multiple parks at a large discount.
Price: $353 for Adults (10+), $324 for Child (3-9)
Visit www.citypass.com/southern-california to book.
Parks include:

- Disneyland and Disney California Adventure 3-Day Park Hopper (with Magic Morning)
- SeaWorl
- LEGOLAND California
- Optional add-on to the San Diego Zoo or Safari Park for $42 adult / $34 child

AAA.com

Members save on multi-day tickets and park hoppers.

MagicGuidebooks.com

Our website announces the best deals on discounted tickets and vacation packages as they become available. Sign up for our free e-mail newsletter to get information on discounts directly to your inbox!

Annual Passports

The Disneyland Resort offers 4 annual passports to both parks. Passholders receive discounts on dining and merchandise.

Available Annual Passes

Disney Southern California Select Passport
$339
Covers about half of the year, but excludes weekends and is exclusive to those living in Southern California

Disney Southern California Passport
$469
Includes Sundays and some holidays, that the Southern Californian Select doesn't

Disney Deluxe Passport
$619
More days than the Southern California Passports, however, this pass is available to anyone

Disney Signature Passport
$849
Most days are available with this pass as well as included parking

Disney Signature Plus Passport
$1,049
Year-round admission to both parks any day of the year and included parking

More Information: https://disneyland.disney.go.com/passes

CHAPTER SIX

TRAVELING TO THE RESORT

Introduction

With the planning out of the way, it's time to being your vacation to the Disneyland Resort. Getting there doesn't have to be tricky, but if you don't plan correctly, it might feel like a complicated mess. Again, we're here to help and simplify!

Contrary to what many believe, Disneyland is not in Los Angeles. The Resort is located in Anaheim, California, which is about 25-30 miles south of Los Angeles (a 45-minute drive from the LAX Airport). However, it is easy to travel from Los Angeles to Disneyland and back in a day.

In this chapter, we review the different methods of getting to the resort. How you get there is entirely up to you, but if you're feeling indecisive (or just need more information to choose), read thoroughly to get the best choices.

By Airline

If you aren't planning a road trip and live far away the Disneyland Resort, flying will likely be your best option. While airlines can be expensive at times, we there are several ways to save money:

1. Compare airlines to see the best pricing

2. Check baggage fees and allowed carry-on items. We prefer Southwest because they give you 2 free checked bags

3. Book early to get the best discounts

<u>Fly into LAX</u> (Los Angeles International):
We recommend LAX because it tends to be the least expensive and easiest to travel from. LAX is located right next to highways that will take you to Disneyland.

By Car

Whether it's a road trip, staying in a neighboring city, or you live close enough to drive to the resort, this can be a great method to take in the beautiful sights of California before you head to the Happiest Place on Earth!

Car Rental: We recommend Enterprise.com or Dollar.com for car rental as they typically have great selection and the best pricing. Pre-booking before you arrive at the airport is advised:

Popular Car Rental Companies:

- www.Enterprise.com: You can visit the company's website or see typically better deals on Priceline.com (or bundle with your airfare and hotel booking)
- www.Dollar.com: click the "specials" tab for deals
- www.Budget.com: click the "deals" tab for offers.

The Easy Drive to Disneyland from LAX (45 minutes):

1. Follow the signs to I-105 East
2. Take I-105 East to I-5 South
3. Take I-5 South to Disneyland Drive
4. Once on Disneyland Drive, follow the signs to available parking (depending on the time you get to the resort will also depend on which parking is available)
5. Resort Parking costs $20 (though this can change throughout the year). Parking at Downtown Disney can cost three times as much and you aren't supposed to park there if you are visiting the parks. Hotel guests pay separately and park closer to their hotel. For $35, you can select preferred parking though this won't get you much closer to the park and we rarely recommend it unless you show up on very busy days and have lots of items like strollers.
6. Take note of where you parked so that you can easily find your spot again when you leave!

Notes:

1. *We recommend using a GPS navigation app that can help you potentially avoid traffic hotspots. With heavy traffic, this route may not be the best.*
2. *Sometimes driving to finding parking at the Disneyland Resort can be a bit confusing. Follow the signs as best as you can to ensure that you find parking in a lot or a parking structure.*
3. *If you've chosen another airport, follow the steps above but I-5 will be your ticket to entering the Disneyland Resort. From San Diego, the northbound carpool lane also empties straight onto Disneyland Drive.*

By Shuttle

The Disneyland Resort Express can take you from the airport to Disneyland (LAX and John Wayne Airports only). The shuttle also drops off at most of the resort hotels and the surrounding hotels properties. Visit www.graylineanahiem.com to book

- From LAX: *$48 roundtrip/adult* *$30 one way/adult*
- From John Wayne Airport (Orange County):

$30 roundtrip/adult *$20 one way/adult*

- For each airport, kids under 11 are free with each paying adult. You must order the tickets together for this promotion.
- Look for the Disneyland Express signs in the airport.
- It is highly recommended that you purchase in advance for the best deals and to ensure seating.
- Departures leave throughout the day. Check the website for times before booking.

By Train

Taking the train can a be relaxing and beautiful way to travel to the Disneyland Resort. Trains let out at the Anaheim Station about 2.5 from the Disneyland Resort. You will need to a second transport from the train station to the resort (we recommend a rideshare service like Uber).

- **Amtrak** - Perfect for longer distances.
  Website: www.Amtrak.com
  Check the "Deals" tab for discounts.
- **Metrolink** - Better pricing for shorter distances

(from the south of Anaheim)
  Website: www.metrolinktrains.com

By Private Car App

With ride-sharing apps like Uber and Lyft taking off, it may seem like a top choice. Both of these services offer private drivers in clean cars (these are not cabs). Here are a few ways you can book:

Uber or Lyft (mobile application):
To download one of these applications, open the App Store (Apple Devices) or Play Store (Android Devices) and search the application by its name.

- These applications will start you at approximately $35-$40 each way (depending on traffic).
- Lyft tends to be less expensive while Uber has a better selection of high-end cars and private options for a premium price.
- Promo codes (typically only for first time riders):
    - Uber: uber.com/promo (often a free ride)

Notes:

1. *Uber doesn't require a tip, and Lyft allows you to. You don't have to tip on these apps and the drivers won't ask you for one.*
2. *The estimated costs are just that - estimations. The time of day and traffic does matter. In the app you can select an estimated fare by entering your destination.*

By Town Car or Taxi

www.Limos.com- an affordable way to take a private town car, limo, or van for special occasions and large groups. $10 off promo code from airports: AFF$10.

www.Taxi.com - hail a taxi and ask for a flat rate. These are the typical prices.

- LAX: $100 each way
- Burbank Airport: $100 each way
- Ontario Airport: $100 each way
- John Wayne Airport: $45 each way
- Long Beach Airport: $45 each way

Note: *It is customary to tip your cab driver 15-20%, depending on your experience with the drive.*

Rent a Car - Hertz is the closest to the train station. Visit Hertz.com for early booking your car (check the "Discounts & Coupons" tab for deals).

By Taxi - cabs often wait in front of the station. They tend to be a little bit more expensive than Uber or Lyft and you are encouraged to tip.

CHAPTER SEVEN

WHAT TO WEAR AND BRING

Introduction

Now that you've planned your vacation, it's time to figure out what to bring and wear! Here we explain how to maximize your fun through comfortable clothing and bringing the right items. Disneyland forbids certain, everyday items, but also permits other items you may assume are banned. For instance, you can bring your own water into the park. This can be extremely helpful because a bottle of water at the Disneyland Parks more than $3! In this section, we review tips and tricks for a comfortable and cost-effective stay at the resort.

Note: *Be aware that the Disneyland Resort inspects your bags before you enter the parks.*

What to Wear and Bring

1. **Comfortable Clothing** - Shorts, t-shirts, sneakers (trainers), and tank tops are seen all around the parks for a good reason: they are comfortable. You'll be standing in the warm California sun all day, so we recommend that you dress comfortably.

2. **Hats and Sunglasses** - Again, the California sun! It's a wonderful thing, but you don't want to get burned. Be careful of hats and sunglasses on rides (most high-speed attractions will have a compartment to store your items).

3. **Sunscreen** - Even on a cloudy day the ultraviolet rays from the sun can give you an uncomfortable burn. Be careful and stay protected.

4. **Stroller** - Kids can get tired and Disneyland has zones to park these with attendants that watch them while you ride.

5. **A Jacket or Sweater** - Even on a hot day the Disneyland Resort can get chilly at night. We highly recommend having a jacket or sweater to keep you warm.

6. **Water Bottles** - Disneyland will allow you to bring sealed bottles of water into the parks. Save yourself money and bring your own. If you don't mind fountain water, you can refill at water fountains near any restroom for free.

7. **Snacks** - You can save money (or help any picky eaters in your party) by bringing your own snacks.

8. **A Waterproof Cellphone Bag** - If you plan on riding the water attractions like Splash Mountain or Grizzly River Run, you're likely to get soaked. The last thing you want is to accidently drench your cellphone! Either purchase a waterproof bag (we recommend the FRiEQ case bags that are sold on Amazon.com) or bring a sandwich baggie.

9. **A School-Sized Backpack** - Carry your items in one of these. Make sure it's not too large to fit on the rides. Also keep in mind that your bag will be checked by security before entering the park area.

10. **Money** - The Disneyland Resort accepts all major credit cards and cash. For currency exchange, visit City Hall (Disneyland), Chamber of Commerce (California Adventure), or any resort hotel front desk.

11. **Identification** - For adults, make sure you plan on bringing your government-issued ID if you plan to drink alcoholic beverages.

12. **Rainy Days** - It doesn't rain much at the Disneyland Resort (only around 12 inches of rainfall in a year), but just in case it does, compact umbrellas and ponchos are great ways to stay dry.

Note: *For information about what to bring for babies and toddlers, please see our Tips for Visiting with Kids chapter later in this book. We detail everything that you'll need and backup plans for when you forget items.*

What *Not* to Wear or Bring

1. **Selfie Sticks** - It seems like it would be so much fun, but Disneyland bans them for the safety of other guests.

2. **Adult Costumes and Masks** - Children under 14 are allowed to wear costumes, but as not to trick people into think a non-Cast Member is a character, Disneyland bans these for adults. During Mickey's Halloween Party, you may dress in costume.

3. **Skateboards, Rollerblades, Bikes, Roller skates** - Disneyland bans these for safety reasons. Even those skates that slide out from kids' shoes are banned. If you need a vehicle, you may rent a scooter or wheelchair from Guest Services to the right of the Disneyland entrance gates.

4. **Remote Control Toys and Drones**

5. **Your Pet** - The Disneyland Resort Kennel Club offers daily service for $20 per pet. Keep in mind that you will need to feed your pet during the day and they don't provide overnight stays. Call (714) 781-7662 for details. If you need require overnight accommodations for your dog, Camp Bow Wow is about 15 minutes from the resort: campbowwow.com/anaheim

6. **Alcoholic Beverages** - These are not allowed in the parks (though you may purchase alcoholic drinks at Disney California Adventure and Downtown Disney).

7. **Lawn Chairs** - You might be tempted to bring these to watch a parade, but Disneyland bans them. We assume it's to keep the resort's aesthetics away from looking like a 4th of July picnic.

8. **Glass Bottles** - Another safety precaution. However, small glass containers of baby food are allowed.

9. **Bags with Wheels and Hiking Backpacks**

10. **Wrapped Gifts** - For inspection reasons, you cannot bring wrapped gifts into the park. Gifts, however, may be wrapped once you enter the park.

Backup Plans

Rent a Locker - We suggest renting a locker to everyone. There's no need to tire yourself out with a hefty backpack when a locker that fits your belongings starts at just $7 for a day rental. Lockers are located just outside of each park gate. Disneyland's are located on Main Street and California Adventure's are located Buena Vista Street

Plan a Midday Return to Your Hotel - If you don't want to rent a locker, make a plan to return to your hotel midday. There you can eat, refill on drinks, and maybe take a power nap before heading back to the parks.

★ **Magic Tip** ★
If you forget any of these items, Disneyland sells them. Check the Main Street, U.S.A., Buena Vista Street, and Downtown Disney shops for any items that you may need.

CHAPTER EIGHT

HOTEL GUIDE

Introduction

As you near the property of the Disneyland Resort, one of the first things you'll notice are the collections of hotels near the entrance. The City of Anaheim has a bit of a mid-century charm set in suburbia (and is heavily influenced by the parks), and the hotels reflect this appeal.

Since there are so many hotels, inns, and motels, it may be very difficult for you to choose where to stay. Ultimately, the choice comes down to staying on or off the resort - followed by *which* hotel to reserve your room with.

In this chapter, we outline the pros and cons of staying off and on the Disneyland Resort. We give you our recommendations, hotel details, and tips for saving on booking to help you make your decision with ease.

Should I Stay On or Off Resort?

The Disneyland Resort offers three amazing hotels, each with a different theme. The most luxurious is Disney's Grand Californian Hotel and Spa, followed by the classic Disneyland Hotel, and the more affordable Disney's Paradise Pier Hotel. Keep in mind that none of these properties run cheap. Since they have exclusive access to the parks, extended park hours, and many more surprises, we recommend staying on resort property.

However, it's not necessary to stay on property. Many more affordable hotels are within walking distance of the resort. These properties may offer nice rooms, pools, breakfast, and sometimes a views of Disneyland from your room. All of this while potentially saving you hundreds of dollars (or *thousands*, depending on your length of stay).

Tips for Booking Discounts on Hotels

1. When you book online at Disneyland.com or over the phone, you can often just put $200 down on a reservation (this includes any bundled park tickets and added items) and pay the remaining balance closer to your arrival date.
2. Always check third party travel websites for better deals (i.e.: Orbitz.com, Bookit.com, Expedia.com) and compare to the Disneyland website.
3. Sometimes you can save quite a bit per night with third-party websites. Click on their "deals" or "promotions" tab to find discount coupons on the sites.

4. Though many websites offer packaged deals, sometimes these are not the lowest cost. We recommend checking the pricing of hotels and flights separately before you commit to a vacation package.
5. Seasonally, Disneyland.com will offer discounted hotel pricing (usually 20-30% off). We recommended booking early when you see these deals!

Disneyland Resort Properties

There are three hotel properties on the resort, each with their own unique sense of themed magic from a wilderness lodge to a beachside hotel. There's something for everyone here, but sometimes it's hard to decide since each has its perks, whether it's the amenities, the views, or the overcall cost.

Benefits of Staying at a Disneyland Resort Hotel

1. Closest proximity to the parks (save on walking time)
2. "Extra Magic Hours" get hotel guests in the park earlier (or later) than anyone else on select dates
3. Private entrance for guests of all 3 hotels through the Grand Californian Hotel to Disney California Adventure.
4. Walking distance to the restaurants, shops, and fun of Downtown Disney
5. Free merchandise delivery to your hotel from any of the Disney shops in the parks. The following day you can pick them up from the bell services in your hotel.
6. Gorgeous pools with waterslides
7. Disney Character Wake-Up Calls from one of your favorites. Kids love this!
8. Free Wi-Fi

The Disneyland Hotel Overview

1150 Magic Way, Anaheim, CA 92802
Booking: **www.Disneyland.com** or call (714) 778-6600
Star Rating: 4

The Disneyland Hotel is our top choice because of its pure-Disney appeal and location at the end of Downtown Disney. Opened in 1955, every piece from the lobby design to the hotel décor, you instantly immersed in Walt Disney's magic.

Pros

- Elegantly designed rooms and suites that bring Disney and mid-century elegance seamlessly together
- Large pool with two monorail-themed water slides and the smaller D-Ticket pool
- Trader Sam's Enchanted Tiki Bar with top-notch cocktails and American bar food. For those wishing that Disneyland had a bar, this is what you've been looking for! When you order special drinks, the entire bar changes, erupting with volcanoes or thunder and lightning - they don't call Trader Sam's an "enchanted" tiki bar for nothing!
- E-Ticket Club-Level option available with continental breakfast, sodas, snacks, desserts, evening wine and cheese, and more. You can even view the fireworks display from the club room.
- Typically, less expensive than the Grand Californian. We also like the design of the Disneyland Hotel standard rooms more than we do the Grand Californian standard rooms. They have a better Disney feel and theme.
- Close to Downtown Disney attractions, restaurants, and shopping

Cons

- Further than the Grand Californian. Since the Disneyland Hotel is located at the opposite end of Downtown Disney from the theme parks, it may be a little of bit of a pain walking there. However, the monorail is always a fast solution that departs out of Tomorrowland to the Disneyland Hotel.
- The Disneyland Hotel is a premium destination that comes with a premium price. A less expensive alternative would be the Paradise Pier Hotel or a hotel outside of the resort.

Disney's Grand Californian Hotel and Spa

1600 Disneyland Dr., Anaheim, CA 92802
Booking: www.Disneyland.com or call (714) 778-6600
Star Rating: 4

A visitor favorite, Disney's Grand Californian brings luxury to the Disneyland Resort. The hotel opened just before Disney California Adventure in 2001 and is designed after hotels in Northern California (if you've ever been to the Ahwahnee Hotel in Yosemite, it has a similar magnificent appeal). The standard rooms have recently gone through an elegant remodel.

Pros

- It's beautiful! Hotel guest will be stunned when entering the grand lobby of this magnificent hotel.
- Freshly updated guest rooms and pool area as of 2017!
- The closest hotel to the resort with a private entrance to the Disney California Adventure for its guest. This is our favorite feature, especially since the entrance is by the Grizzly River Run, so it makes a great stopping point if you need to change after getting soaked!
- Elegantly designed rooms and suites with a lodge feel.
- Three pools: The Fountain Pool, Redwood Pool with water slide, and the Mariposa Pool for relaxing. Poolside Cabanas available at the Mariposa Pool.
- Spa that offers massages, facials, and other treatments.
- Close to Downtown Disney attractions, restaurants, and shopping.

Cons

- The Grand Californian is a luxury destination that comes with a luxury price. It is often the most expensive of three Disneyland Resort hotels.
- The newly remodeled standard rooms are still missing some of the classic Disney appeal found in the artwork and details of the Disneyland Hotel rooms. This may not be an issue if you're not interested in being surrounded by Disney every waking moment

Disney's Paradise Pier Hotel

1717 Disneyland Dr., Anaheim, CA 92802
Booking: www.Disneyland.com or call (714) 778-6600
Star Rating: 4

The Paradise Pier may be the lowest priced hotel on the resort, but it's still a premium stay with splendid rooms. In fact, Paradise Pier has generally the largest room sizes of any of the resorts. Many families with children enjoy staying here because of the low cost and extra square footage.

Pros:

- Stylishly designed rooms and suites themed as a 1920s beachfront hotel
- The lowest price of the three resort hotels
- Typically, the largest rooms of the three resort hotels
- Rooftop pools with the Paradise Spa whirlpool, a children's pool, and a waterslide in the Paradise Pool
- The Surfside Lounge serves cocktails for adults 21 and up
- Close to Downtown Disney attractions, restaurants, and shopping
- See the fireworks from the pool deck on select nights.

Cons:

- The furthest hotel in the resort from the parks. Disney's Paradise Pier Hotel is still close to the end of Downtown Disney and near the Disneyland. Therefore, the walking distance from the theme parks to the hotel might be a bit of a trek. To avoid this, we recommend taking the monorail out of Tomorrowland to the Disneyland Hotel. The Paradise Pier is just a short walking distance away from there.
- The hotel is missing some of the magic felt in the other two resort hotels. The Paradise Pier Hotel feels more like a standard hotel without the grandiose lobbies. However, the rooms don't disappoint Disney lovers with their themed décor.

Mores Reasons to Stay on Resort

Hotel Parking: You still have to pay for this but the parking is much closer than the rest of the resort and you can leave your vehicle overnight (check Disneyland.com for details on cars and oversized vehicles as they are subject to change). Valet is also available at an additional cost.

Disney Power Walks: Walks through Disneyland are offered to hotel guests beginning at 6AM. Check with the Guest Services Desk at your resort hotel for details.

Laundry: You may have your clothes dry cleaned or laundered Monday through Saturday. Perfect for those traveling long, staying extendedly, or stopping by during a business trip. The Grand Californian has its own laundry room for self-service.

Breakfast with Disney Characters: Fun for the kid in all of us and delicious food from eggs and bacon to pancakes and fresh-made omelets. These are located right inside of the hotel, so you can always head back to the room for a refresh before heading to the parks.

<u>Character Dining Hotel Locations</u>

- Disneyland Hotel: Goofy's Kitchen
- Grand Californian: Storytellers Café
- Paradise Pier: PCH Grill

⋆ **Magic Tip** ⋆

Check <u>Disneyland.com</u> for dining times and to reserve your spot early. Non-hotel guests can also reserve and dine.

Recommended Hotels Outside of the Resort

For those looking to save money, staying at the Disneyland Resort Hotels may not be an option. The good news is there are several hotels nearby that offer transportation or are within walking distance.

1. **Courtyard Marriott Anaheim Theme Park Entrance**
   Star Rating: 3
   Price: Moderate
   Distance: 5-minute walk to the Disneyland Resort
   Pool: Yes
   Perks: Close to the theme parks, pool with waterslides, certain rooms have resort views
   Contact: (714) 254-1442 / www.marriott.com

2. **The Anabella**
   Star Rating: 3
   Price: Moderate
   Distance: 5-minute walk to the Disneyland Resort
   Pool: Yes
   Perks: Classic hotel at a great price, certain rooms have resort views
   Contact: (800) 863-4888 / www.anabellahotel.com (check the promotions tab for deals)

3. **Hyatt Regency Orange County**
   Star Rating: 4
   Price: Moderate
   Distance: 1 mile walk to the Disneyland Resort / also offers shuttles for $5 each adult
   Pool: Yes (2)
   Perks: Beautiful, premium hotel near the convention center

Contact: (714) 750-1234 / orangecounty.hyatt.com (click the "offers" tab for deals)

4. **Best Western Plus Park Place Inn**
   Star Rating: 2.5
   Price: Economic
   Distance: 5-minute walk to the Disneyland Resort
   Pool: Yes
   Perks: Free breakfast, inexpensive, and walking distance!
   Contact: (714) 776-4800 / www.bestwestern.com (check the "Offers" tab for deals including senior, AAA, and government).

5. **Candy Cane Inn**
   Star Rating: 2
   Price: Economic
   Distance: 5-10 walk to the Disneyland Resort
   Pool: Yes (2)
   Perks: Classic inn feel with free breakfast and coffee
   Contact: (714) 774-5284 / www.candycaneinn.net (check the website for promo codes)

6. **Del Sol Inn**
   Star Rating: 2
   Price: Economic
   Distance: 5-minute walk to the Disneyland Resort
   Pool: Yes
   Perks: Classic inn feel that is very close to the resorts
   Contact: (888) 686-1122 / www.delsolinn.com (click the promotions tab for deals)

CHAPTER NINE
DISNEYLAND PARK

Introduction

When we know that a friend or family member is going to visit Disneyland, we become excited for them. We love offering tips and ideas for attractions to make their visit even better. Disneyland is the original world-class theme park that opened its gates over 60 years ago, in July of 1955. With more than 60 rides and attractions across 8 lands (Main Street, U.S.A., Adventureland, Frontierland, New Orleans Square, Critter Country, Fantasyland, Mickey's Toontown, and Tomorrowland) the Disneyland Park has something for everyone.

In this chapter, we review the magical park that started it all! Disneyland has an undeniable charm that will come over you, bringing you into the wonderful world of Walt Disney.

Main Street, U.S.A.

Disneyland's iconic grand entrance is filled with shops, dining, and a magnificent view of the castle. The first thing you'll notice is the train station, beautiful flower arrangements, and smiling faces. Choose the left or the right side of the entrance to find yourself in a hub of horse-drawn street cars, carriages, unique shops, and Disney characters waiting to greet you. At night, Main Street U.S.A. becomes the center for the Disneyland fireworks show.

Theme: Turn-of-the-century American town – specifically, Walt Disney's hometown of Marceline, Missouri in the early 20th century

★ **Magic Tips** ★

1. Main Street makes a great viewing spot for many of the parades and nighttime fireworks displays. Crowds line up along the streets typically 30 minutes before each show to get a great view. If you'd like to avoid the parades and shows, it's best to stay clear of Main Street around these show times.
2. Get souvenirs here on your way out of the park. They have everything from character antennae balls and other trinkets to clothing and specialty candy!
3. Rent a locker here if you need space to store your things (they start at $7 for rental the entire day). Lockers are located behind the fruit stand on the right side as you walk toward the castle.

Rides

Main Street Vehicles

Description: Ride a horse-drawn streetcar, horseless carriage, or a double-decker bus that will take you down to Sleeping Beauty Castle.

Level: Family

Recommendation: A nice stroll for small children and guests who enjoy the classic appeal of Disney attractions. However, thrill riders might rather skip this and head straight to a ride like Space Mountain.

FastPass: None

Disneyland Railroad

Description: a railroad that moves around the perimeter of the park and makes stops in New Orleans Square, Fantasyland/Toontown, and Tomorrowland.

Level: Everyone

Recommendation: Fun if you'd like an easy way to ride from town to town. If you take the railroad all around the perimeter of the park, you will see surprises like volcanoes and dinosaurs!

FastPass: None

Shows and Attractions

Mickey's Soundsational Parade

Description: See Mickey and his friends dance to to beat-driven music as they march down Main Street and Fantasyland on vibrant floats in this popular parade!

Level: Young Kids, Kids

Recommendation: A perfect midday break for families with young kids

FastPass: None

"Fantasy In the Sky" Fireworks

Disneyland's stunning classic fireworks display. Watch the magic all around the park as fireworks set off behind Sleeping Beauty Castle.

★ **Magic Tips** ★

- The best viewing is on Main Street, U.S.A. as the projections light up the buildings all around you.
- The fireworks go off behind the castle, so the closer you are to the castle, the larger they will appear.
- If you are staying the Disneyland Hotel or the Paradise Pier, they offer special rooftop firework viewing from the property. This is especially great if you wish to avoid the crowds.
- Staying at the Grand Californian? Ask the concierge how you can enjoy private hotel firework shows.

Great Moments with Mr. Lincoln

Description: A classic animatronic show starring the sixteenth President of the United States, Abraham Lincoln.

Level: Everyone

Recommendation: Perfect for guests who love the nostalgia of Walt Disney's animatronic storytelling. Personally, we love this attraction for its music, historical detail, and the fun of seeing Abraham Lincoln come to life. However, thrill-seekers and restless children will likely want to skip this one.
FastPass: None

Even More:
You can also discover the many shops, City Hall, the Main Street Cinema playing classic Disney Studio animated shorts, and the Disneyland Gallery.

Adventureland

Theme: Enter the jungle, explore ruins, and ride the Indiana Jones Adventure in this lush and beautifully landscaped attraction area.

Rides

Indiana Jones Adventure
Description: travel through a hidden jungle temple and hop aboard a classic jeep-like vehicle that holds up to 12 passengers.
Level: Thrill Ride (must be 46"/117cm or taller)
Recommendation: This is a unique ride that is only at Disneyland and it should not be missed by thrill riders.

FastPass: Available to the left of the entrance.

★ **Magic Tips** ★

1. Indiana Jones gets flak for having the "worst FastPass". Simply put, the FastPass option only skips the outside line and rarely parts of the inside. Because of this, we don't recommend FastPass for Indiana Jones unless the standard wait time is an 45 minutes or more, which it often is.
2. On a crowded day, ask the Cast Member at the entrance of the ride (typically dressed like Indiana Jones) about the "Single Rider Line" - you will receive a pass to cut through the bulk of the line and you will likely not sit with the rest of your party when boarding. Sometimes this option is not faster, though is usually is.
3. In the spike chamber in the queue, look for a bamboo pole. Shake it until you hear the room rumble and the spikes fall from above.
4. Look for a "don't pull the rope" sign in the queue above the well. Do it and hear the person below yell for help!

Jungle Cruise

Description: Venture down a massive river on a boat with your tour comedic tour guide. See animatronic Amazonian and African animals from monkeys and crocodiles to elephants and lions on this 7-minute long ride.

Level: Everyone

Recommendation: A classic, humorous Disneyland ride that most guests will enjoy. Thrill riders may want to skip it.

FastPass: None

★ Magic Tip ★

The holiday version, Jingle Cruise (November - December) offers Christmas lights, a different script, and animals wearing Christmas hats.

Tarzan's Treehouse

Description: Climbable treehouse themed after Disney's Tarzan animated film

Level: Young Kids / Everyone

Recommendation: Kids ages 10 and under will love this attraction that typically has a very short line (or no wait at all).

FastPass: None

★ **Magic Tips** ★

1. One of the best photo opportunities is here. Climb to the top and take a photo at the top for something stunning to share.

Shows and Attractions

Enchanted Tiki Room

Description: An animatronic show starring birds and Tikis in a tropical island setting.

Level: Family / Everyone

Recommendation: Have a Dole Whip while you watch the 15-minute long show. Thrill-seekers will want to skip this one, as it's a classic attraction that can feel a bit dated.

FastPass: None

Aladdin's Oasis

Description: *Aladdin*-themed show and "On-The-Go" meals.

Type: "On-The-Go" service (take the meal with you)

Price: $$

Recommendation: Lasagna Bolognese

★ **Magic Tip** ★

You can get the best viewing for the fireworks when eating at Aladdin's Oasis. Visit Disneyland.com (or call 714-781-DINE) to book your reservation up to 60 days in advance.

Frontierland

Theme: Immerse yourself in the wild west near the Rivers of America. Ride the high-speed Big Thunder Mountain Railroad or catch a lighthearted show at the Golden Horseshoe Stage.

Rides

Big Thunder Mountain Railroad
Description: A fast rollercoaster with a few dips called "The Wildest Ride in the Wilderness"!
Level: Thrill Ride (must be 40"/102cm or taller)
Recommendation: Many families and thrill riders will love this fast rollercoaster with short dips and great special effects.
FastPass: Available near the entrance.

• **Mark Twain Riverboat** - Explore a beautiful American-style riverboat.

• **Frontierland Shootin' Exposition** - A paid experience where you can shoot targets with laser-guided rifles.

• **Pirate's Lair on Tom Sawyer Island** - Board a raft and set sail for an island playground perfect for Kids and Tweens.

• **Sailing Ship Columbia** - A massive 18th-century themed boat that sails guest around the Rivers of America.

• **Davy Crockett's Explorer Canoes** - don't come with your arms sore! Guests paddle down the Rivers of American in Frontierland while seeing the stunning waterscape of Disneyland.

Shows and Attractions

The Golden Horseshoe Stage

Description: A family-friendly saloon-style show and dining experience.
Level: Family / Everyone
Recommendation: Western-style show with songs and jokes while you dine. Walt Disney himself loved this attraction!
FastPass: None

New Orleans Square

Theme: A southern America-themed land filed with shops, treats, and a couple of very famous rides including Pirates of the Caribbean and the Haunted Mansion. Dine on creole favorites or catch the stunning nighttime show, Fantasmic!

Rides

Pirates of the Caribbean

Description: Pirate-themed boat ride in the dark
Level: Everyone
Recommendation: A must-see Disney Classic for all!
FastPass: None
★ **Magic Tips** ★

1. Hack the line! When facing the entrance, the line on the right is typically the shortest as there is less queue than the left side.
2. A great air conditioned ride to cool off on warm days.

Haunted Mansion

Description: A slow-paced ride through a haunted house.
Level: Everyone (though young children may become frightened)

Recommendation: It's a Disneyland classic that many thrill-riders may want to skip for it's slow movement and effects that are only scary enough to terrify young children. However, if it's in the Holiday season (mid-September through December), we highly recommend the Haunted Mansion Holiday (themed after Tim Burton's *The Nightmare Before Christmas*), with added special effects and animatronics.
FastPass: Available near the entrance

Shows and Attractions

Fantasmic!

Description: An epic nighttime spectacular over the Rivers of America. Displays music and scenes from Disney classic films brought to life with special effects, actors, and floats!
Level: Family / Everyone
Recommendation: A perfect nighttime spectacular for show fans.
FastPass: Yes
★ **Magic Tip** ★
Get a FastPass for Fantasmic! at the start of your day. This won't prevent you from getting other FastPasses as it is "disconnected" from the rest.

Critter Country

Theme: A backwoods and forest-themed land, home of Splash Mountain.

Rides

Splash Mountain
Description: Water-based log ride starring the singing critters from the classic Disney film "Song of the South"
Level: Thrill (must be 40"/102cm or taller)
Recommendation: If you love getting wet and drops, this is the ride for you!
FastPass: Available
★ **Magic Tips** ★

1. This ride typically has the longest lines on hot, Summer days. A FastPass is highly recommended.
2. Sit near the back to avoid getting as wet (though you will still likely get wet). Ask a Cast Member at the end of the line to sit in the back and they will help accommodate you.
3. If you want to get soaked - ask a Cast Member to sit in the front!
4. If it's a cold day or you just don't feel like getting your clothes wet, either buy/bring a poncho or skip this attraction (though it is one of our favorites).
5. Say cheese! The camera for Splash Mountain is on the right side of the boat as you plunge down the last drop.

The Many Adventures of Winnie the Pooh

Description: A slow-paced ride through the brightly-colored world of Winnie the Pooh.

Level: Young Kids / Family

Recommendation: Great for small kids, but teens and thrill-riders will want to skip.

FastPass: None

★ ★ ★ ★ ★ ★ ★ ★ ★ ★ ★ ★ ★

Fantasyland

Theme: Magic makes memories in this classic kid-friendly land located behind the famous castle.

Rides

Matterhorn Bobsleds

Description: Swiss mountain-themed rollercoaster and Fantasyland's only thrill ride.

Level: Thrill (must be 42"/107cm or taller)

Recommendation: Board the left side (there are two tracks)

FastPass: Yes

★ **Magic Tip** ★

> There are two separate tracks for the Matterhorn and they are slightly different. The one track loads on the left (when you are looking at the mountain from the loading sides) is a bit faster than the other. The other side is better for those not looking for great speed.

Peter Pan's Flight

Description: Fly along Peter Pan through London and Neverland on a pirate ship!

Level: Young Kids / Everyone

Recommendation: Perfect for all ages and a Disneyland classic that we even recommend to thrill-seekers.

FastPass: None

★ **Magic Tip** ★

> Peter Pan's Flight can have one of the longest lines in the park. To avoid these, we recommend riding this first if you are with small children who may have short attention spans.

Dumbo the Flying Elephant

Description: Soar high while boarding Dumbo! Also hold a feather to help Dumbo take off.

Level: Young Kids / Everyone

Recommendation: Perfect for families with young children.

FastPass: None

★ **Magic Tip** ★

> This attraction typically has very long lines and is a short ride. The only way to limit this is to get to Disneyland at the park's opening and ride Dumbo early.

Alice in Wonderland

Description: Hop aboard the Caterpillar and see the whimsical story of Walt Disney's *Alice in Wonderland*.

Level: Kids / Everyone

Recommendation: Perfect families with kids of all ages. This classic dark ride is also popular amongst Disneyland fans with its charming characters, glow-in-the-dark lightning effects, and even newly added magic!

FastPass: None

Mad Tea Party (Tea Cups)

Description: Disneyland's famous tea cups inspired by Alice in Wonderland! Spin with your friends (up to 3-4 adults per tea cup).

Level: Kids / Everyone

Recommendation: Perfect for all ages and a Disneyland classic that we even recommend to thrill-seekers (the tea cups can spin *fast* or slow, depending on how hard you turn them).

FastPass: None

★ **Magic Tip** ★

Rumor has it that the FASTEST spinning one is the plain purple teacup (not the one with the flowers).

Mr. Toad's Wild Ride

Description: Zip in a zany buggy that follows the story of Mr. Toad (from the 1949 animated film, *The Adventures of Ichabod and Mr. Toad*).

Level: Kids / Family

Recommendation: Perfect for all ages. It's a Disneyland-only classic ride (Disney World closed this attraction in 1998 and replaced it with the Many Adventures of Winnie the Pooh).

FastPass: None

Snow White's Scary Adventures

Description: Travel through the tale of *Snow White and the Seven Dwarfs*

Level: Kids / Family

Recommendation: Perfect for families with young children.

FastPass: None

★ **Magic Tip** ★

Look up at the window above the Snow White ride. You will see the Evil Queen pull the curtains back every few minutes to greet you!

Pinocchio's Daring Journey

Description: A slow-paced, but colorful ride that follows the story of Walt Disney's *Pinocchio*.

Level: Kids / Family

Recommendation: Perfect for families with young children.

FastPass: None

King Arthur Carrousel

Description: A classic carrousel with horses from *The Sword in the Stone*

Level: Kids / Family

Recommendation: Perfect for families with young children.

FastPass: None

Casey Jr. Circus Train

Description: Pretend you're a circus animal on this slow-paced train that takes you up and down the hills from the movie *Dumbo*.

Level: Kids / Family

Recommendation: Perfect for families with young children.

FastPass: None

Storybook Land Canal Boats

Description: A boat ride through Monstro the Whale's mouth views of miniature models of Disney's best movies.

Level: Kids / Family

Recommendation: Perfect for families with young children.

FastPass: None

Note: *This ride closes during parades.*

"it's a small world"

Description: A boat floats through several counties with children singing the "It's A Small World" theme song in different languages.

Level: Young Kids / Family
Recommendation: Perfect for families with young children. During the holiday season, this ride dazzles with lights and new costumes.
FastPass: None
★ **Magic Tips** ★
Look for characters like Ariel and Aladdin hidden throughout the ride.

Shows and Attractions

Sleeping Beauty Castle Walkthrough
Description: Walk through the Disneyland castle
Level: Family / Everyone
Recommendation: Walk through, see the art, and take a picture outside of the castle.
FastPass: None
★ **Magic Tips** ★

1. There is often a Disneyland photographer outside of the castle. He or she will take your picture for free (though you have to pay for the prints) and afterward, the Cast Member is happy to take a free photo of you with your camera or phone.

Fantasy Faire (with Royal Hall and Royal Theatre)
Description: The newest addition to Fantasyland with shows and treats. Meet Princesses in the Royal Hall and watch them perform lives shows (*Beauty and the Beast* and *Tangled*) in the Royal Theatre.
Level: Kids / Family
Recommendation: Perfect for children of all ages who love Disney Princess with bench seating. Also one of the better spots to take a photo with a Disney princess!
FastPass: None

★ **Magic Tips** ★

1. Maurice's Treats Snack Cart serves some extremely delicious pastries!
2. Get a princess-themed Mickey Hat at the Fairy Tale Treasures Shop.

Bibbidi Bobbidi Boutique

Description: Dress up in princess clothing and makeup

Level: Kids and Young Kids

Recommendation: Perfect for children who are inspired Disney princesses (for pricing starting a $59.95, kids can get their makeup and hair done- and even a gown from their favorite Disney princess). There are more packages, including a "Knight Package" and a "Frozen Package".

Make an appointment up to 60 days in advance by calling (714) 781-7895

FastPass: None

Pixie Hollow

Description: Meet Tinker Bell and her friends between high blades of grass.

Level: Kids and Young Kids

Recommendation: Great for kids the pixie fan of any age

FastPass: None

Fantasyland Theatre Presents: Mickey and the Magical Map

Description: A live action show starring Mickey Mouse and his friends.

Level: Family

Recommendation: Great for show lovers of all ages. Awesome special effects, singing, and dancing.

FastPass: None

Tip: Get there early for the best seating!

★ ★ ★ ★ ★ ★ ★ ★ ★ ★ ★ ★ ★

Mickey's Toontown

Theme: A cartoon town where guests can visit Mickey Mouse and his friends in their homes.

★ **Magic Tips** ★
Toon Town is interactive! Pull the lever near the fireworks and see what happens or take a photo behind the jail cell bars! You can also Pry open crates, ring that door bell, and try to open the doors for big surprises!

Rides

Roger Rabbit's Car Toon Spin
Description: A "dark ride" where riders can spin the wheel and make the car turn on the track.
Level: Everyone
Recommendation: Great for kids and possibly some thrill-riders.
FastPass: Available

Gadget's Go Coaster
Description: A short, kid-friendly rollercoaster
Level: Kids and Young Kids (must be 35"/ 89cm or taller)
Recommendation: Great for kids, unless there is a long wait. This ride is very short and the line is often very long.
FastPass: None
★ **Magic Tip** ★ The seats on this coaster are tiny, so take caution when riding depending on your height/size.

Shows and Attractions

Mickey and Minnie's Houses

Description: Walk through their homes and meet them at the end for a picture!

Level: Family / Everyone

Recommendation: If you want to meet Mickey or Minnie Mouse, this is the best as they aren't often spotted around the parks in their classic clothes.

FastPass: None

Goofy's Playhouse, Donald's Boat, and Chip 'N Dale Treehouse

Description: Play areas with meet and greets with the characters

Level: Kids and Young Kids

Recommendation: great for kids to play and have fun.

FastPass: None

★ **Magic Tip** ★ Goofy is often found in his playhouse and typically will help your child slide down the slide if you ask (great photos!)

Tomorrowland

Theme: World of the Future that is perfect for thrill seekers and more. Tomorrowland is also home to Star Wars-themed attractions from greeting characters like Storm Troopers and Chewbacca to battling evil forces like Darth Vader. You can also blast into hyperspace on Star Tours!

Rides

<u>Space Mountain</u>

Description: Board a rocket ship and blast off into outer space in this classic Disney theme park roller coaster in the dark!

Level: Thrill Riders (must be 40"/ 102cm or taller)

Recommendation: A not-to-be missed attraction for thrill riders and those who love a good roller coaster. Space Mountain has been a Disneyland staple since 1977 and is great fun!

FastPass: Available

★ **Magic Tip** ★

> Get to the park early and grab a FastPass for Space Mountain. Thrill riders tend to like this ride the most and may want to ride it twice.

<u>Star Tours</u> **<u>- The Adventures Continue</u>**

Description: 3D Star Wars-themed motion simulation ride.

Level: Thrill Riders

Recommendation: Perfect for those who enjoy motion simulation rides.

FastPass: Available

Note: *Each time you ride this attraction it's different. Star Tours has nine different planets and a new scene from recent Star Wars films.*

<u>Autopia</u>

Description: Where kids can drive cars around a track.

Level: Kids / Family (must be 32"/81cm or taller to ride) (must be 54"/137cm to drive alone)

Recommendation: Designed for kids to tweens, but with height restrictions.

FastPass: Yes

Finding Nemo Submarine Voyage

Description: Nemo and friends join you underwater in this slow-paced ride filled with animation effects.

Level: Family

Recommendation: Great for all ages, but not for those who may be claustrophobic. Thrill riders may also want to skip this one for its slow pace.

FastPass: None

Buzz Lightyear Astro Blasters

Description: Compete against others in this fun Toy Story themed ride. It seems like it's for the kids, but it's fun for everyone to blast the laser guns and try to rack up the points.

Level: Everyone (including most Thrill Riders)

Recommendation: A crowd favorite with a short line

FastPass: None

⋆ **Magic Tips** ⋆

1. Targets worth the most points are as follows:
    - Blue Diamond targets = 10,000 points
    - Purple Triangles targets = 5,000 points
    - Green Square targets = 1,000 points
    - Circle targets = 100 points
2. You can hit the targets as many times as you'd like (keep hitting the Blue Diamonds!)
3. Targets are worth more when they light up
4. Zurg is worth 50,000 points - if you can hit him! Toward the end of the ride, Emperor Zurg attacks and on his chest is a tiny target. Shoot that small spot and score this extra-big bonus!

Astro Orbiter

Description: Orbit a solar system model on rocket ships (similar to Dumbo)

Level: Kids / Family

Recommendation: Fun for young children
FastPass: None

Shows and Attractions

***Star Wars* Launch Bay**
Description: Take a photo with Chewbacca, Darth Vader, Boba Fett, or Kylo Ren (these characters may change throughout the year). Also see movie props and more.
Level: Family / Everyone
Recommendation: The best place to take a photo with a *Star Wars* character.
FastPass: None
Warning: Kylo Ren and Darth Vader may be too scary for very young children (yes, they are scary and in character!)

Tomorrowland Theater: Path of the Jedi
Description: A 10-minute film that ventures through the *Star Wars* franchise leading up to *The Force Awakens*.
Level: Everyone
Recommendation: Best for big Star Wars fans
FastPass: None

Jedi Training Academy
Description: A stunning showdown between the Jedi and the Sith from *Star Wars*.
Level: Kids / Everyone
Recommendation: Your child could participate and dress as a Jedi to combat Darth Vader is a lightsaber!
FastPass: None
Note: *Located at the stage by the Galactic Grill.*

CHAPTER TEN
DISNEY CALIFORNIA ADVENTURE PARK

Introduction

While Disneyland is the iconic theme park, Disney California Adventure is the cool kid in town! The park opened in 2001 and now is home to 7 California and Pixar-themed lands. With even more Disney-themed rides that aren't found in any other park like the California Screamin' rollercoaster and Mickey's Fun Wheel, California Adventure brings sunny-themed surprises for everyone. Some say that Disney California Adventure is the "adult park" because of its edgier rides and delicious restaurants that serve beer, wine, and specialty cocktails. In fact, those 21 and older can take wine tours and order from full bars all inside of the park.

Thrill riders will love this side of the Disneyland Resort because of its rollercoaster with a loop, dangerous Tower of Terror, and the *Cars*-themed Radiator Springs Racers. However, there's something for everyone in Disney California Adventure from The Little Mermaid "dark ride" to high-flying Soarin'.

Buena Vista Street

Theme: The grand entrance of the park inspired by 1920's Los Angeles when Walt Disney first arrived in California.

Rides

Red Car Trolley
Thrill Level: Everyone
Recommendation: Kids might be fond of this trolley ride to Hollywood Land.
FastPass: None

Paint the Night
A vibrant nighttime parade starring favorite characters from Mickey to Tinker Bell! The spinning lights will catch the eye of everyone around in this state-of-the-art attraction.
Get Preferred Viewing (and beat the crowds):
Book a reservation at select dining locations and receive an "on-the-go" meal as well as preferred seating to Paint the Night. To book, visit Disneyland.com or call (714) 781-4565 up to 60 days in advance.

★ **Magic Tips** ★
We recommend lining up at least 30 minutes before the parade to get the best viewing.

Hollywood Land

Theme: 1920's downtown Hollywood with a back lot, theatre, and animation studio.

Rides

Guardians of the Galaxy - Mission: Breakout

Description: Plummet 13 stories in this Marvel-themed thrill ride.
Level: Thrill riders (must be 40"/ 102cm or taller)
Recommendation: Only for those who love thrilling rides
FastPass: Available
Note: *During Halloween time, mid-September through the end of October, this ride becomes another thrilling experience: Guardians of the Galaxy - Monsters After Dark! The ride is much of the same fun but alien monsters are on the loose and Groot was somehow left behind!*

Monsters, Inc. Mike & Sulley to the Rescue!

Description: Slow moving dark ride
Thrill Level: Kids / Family
Recommendation: Fun for kids and fans of the movie
FastPass: None
⋆ **Magic Tip** ⋆ While Monsters Inc. doesn't have a FastPass, you can get a "buddy pass" to help skip the line instead. This pass gets 2 people into the ride through the exit (Disney has a hard time filling all of the 6-seater cars because of groups of 3-4). Just ask a cast member at the front for the buddy pass.

Shows and Attractions

Disney Animation

Description: A collection of animation-themed attractions

- **Animation Academy** - We highly recommend this unique attraction. A Disney animator shows you how to draw a character in a simple way. The best part is that you can keep your free animation paper!
- **Sorcerer's Workshop** - See how classic Disney animated movies were brought to film and even make a short animation of your own!
- ***Turtle Talk with Crush*** - Interact with Crush the turtle from *Finding Nemo* in this unique and hilarious theatre-like event designed for Young Kids.

Thrill Level: Everyone (Turtle Talk is more for young kids)

Recommendation: Classic Disney

FastPass: None

Note: *Check outside the building for character drawing times*

Frozen - Live at the Hyperion

Description: A live action stage show starring the characters of Frozen. Sing along with Anna, Elsa, and Olaf!

Thrill Level: Family

Recommendation: Any Frozen fan

FastPass: No

Disney Jr. Dance Party

Description: An all-new stage show designed for preschoolers. See their favorite Disney Jr. characters from "The Lion Guard", "Doc McStuffins", "Sofia the First", and "Mickey and the Roadster Racers"!

Thrill Level: Young Kids

Recommendation: Families with very young children only

FastPass: None

a bug's land

Theme: Shrink down into the tall grass for a kid-friendly land themed after Pixar's *A Bug's Life*.

Rides

Flik's Fun Fair

Description: A kids play area with multiple rides:
Level: Young Kids / Family
Recommendation: for the young kids mainly (though many adults enjoy Heimlich's Chew Chew Train for the humor)

- **Heimlich's Chew Chew Train** - our most recommended ride in the zone. Hop aboard a caterpillar-shaped train while Heimlich hilariously guides you through his favorite food to eat. You can even smell the delicious treats!
- **Flik's Flyers** - Move up and down on hot air balloons.
- **Francis' Ladybug Boogie** -ladybug-shaped cars move riders in circles to music.
- **Princess Dot Puddle Park** - jump and splash in this wet zone (⋆ Magic Tip ⋆ this attraction is located next to the restrooms in case you need to dry off).
- **Tuck and Roll's Drive 'Em Buggies** - kid-friendly bumper cars.

Shows and Attractions

<u>It's Tough to be a Bug!</u>

Description: A 4D theatre show themed after Pixar's *A Bug's Life* movie

Thrill Level: Everyone / Family

Recommendation: For those who love 3D movies

FastPass: None

Note: *Often this theatre is changed to premier Disney film previews like with added 4D effects.*

Cars Land

Theme: Route 66 comes to life with Pixar's *Cars*!

⋆ **Magic Tips** ⋆

See the Cars Land Neon Lighting ceremony –a really cool secret that unofficially begins about 5 minutes after sunset right in front of Flo's V9 Café in Cars Land!

Rides

<u>Luigi's Rollickin Roaders</u>

Description: Spin and move to the music in colorful cars. Each time is different!

Level: Kids / Family (must be 32"/ 81cm or taller)

Studio Catering Co. Perfect for kids.

FastPass: None

Radiator Springs Racers

Description: High-Speed Simulated Race Car Ride

Level: Family / Thrill Riders (must be 40"/ 102cm or taller)

Recommendation: Cars Land might seem like it's for little kids, but this ride is for the thrill riders, too.

FastPass: Available

★ **Magic Tips** ★

1. The FastPass for the Radiator Springs Racers is near *It's Tough to be a Bug* and not by the ride itself.
2. Get the FastPass at the beginning of the day. The Radiator Springs Racers passes typically run out *very* early (usually within the first hour of the park opening, even on less crowded days).
3. If you didn't get a FastPass, you may want to opt for the "Single Rider Line". You won't likely sit next to your friends/family (though rarely they will seat you together if 2 spots open), however, the line is much shorter than the regular line. Loading for Single Riders is at the start of the queue to the Radiator Springs Racers in Cars Land.
4. The racers seat up to 6 riders, 3 in each row (similar to Test Track at EPCOT in Walt Disney World).

Mater's Junkyard Jamboree

Description: Get flicked and whirled around while riding the back of Mater's truck.

Level: Kids / Family (must be 32"/ 81cm or taller)

Recommendation: Perfect for kids and thrill riders might also enjoy this unpredictable ride.

FastPass: None

Note: *During Halloween time, mid-September through the end of October, this attraction becomes the family-friendly Halloween ride, Mater's Junkyard JamBOOree and the Rollickin Roadsters become Luigi's Honkin' Haul-O-Ween.*

Paradise Pier

Theme: The central land of Disney California Adventure with a boardwalk-style atmosphere.

Note: *Paradise Pier will be re-themed to Pixar Pier in Summer of 2018 and many of its attractions will likely change names and themes. We expect a lot of construction in this land during the first half of 2018.*

Rides

California Screamin'

Description: A fast steel rollercoaster with big drops and a loop!

Level: Thrill Riders (must be 48"/ 122cm or taller)

Recommendation: The Disneyland Resort's only looped rollercoaster - a thrill rider's dream! Needless to say, it's not for those who don't enjoy intense rollercoasters.

FastPass: Available

★ **Magic Tip** ★

The "Single Rider Line" could save you time on a busy day. Look for the blue sign that says "Single Rider Line" on the left side of the queue (where the ride unloads passengers).

Toy Story Midway Mania!

Description: A 4D game where riders attempt to score the most points by shooting at animated targets with a plunger canon

Level: Everyone

Recommendation: All ages will enjoy this ride, including preschooler, families, and thrill riders. No recommended if you have trouble seeing with 3D glasses.
FastPass: Yes
⋆ **Magic Tips** ⋆ on how to score BIG:

1. Many "pro" riders hold the plunger between two fingers with their palm facing them.
2. Higher-point targets are at the bottom of the screens.
3. Scene #1 (Hamm and Eggs) - Hitting the pigs on the fence will make a cat show that can be hit multiple times for big points.
4. Scene #2 (Rex and Trixie) - Pop the lava balloons on the volcano to make it erupt with 500-point balloons.
5. Scene #3 (Green Army Men) - Look for the yellow-tinted plates that are worth 2,000 points.
6. Scene #4 (Alien Ring Game) - On the far sides are rocket ships and aliens worth big points.
7. Scene #5 (Woody's Western Theme) - Aim for the doors of the saloon to reveal higher point targets. At the end of this scene there are mine carts that roll toward you. Look for the bats above the mine carts that are worth some major points.

King Triton's Carousel
Description: A classic carousel with sea life instead of horses.
Level: Kids / Family
Recommendation: Perfect for kids of all ages.
FastPass: None

The Little Mermaid - Ariel's Undersea Adventure
Description: A family-friendly "dark ride" with bright colors, music, and the story of *The Little Mermaid*.
Level: Young Kids / Kids / Family

Recommendation: Great for families and fans of Disney's *The Little Mermaid*.
FastPass: None

Mickey's Fun Wheel

Description: A massive multi-colored Ferris wheel that has both swinging and stationary gondolas.
Level: Everyone
Recommendation: Thrill riders will love the swinging gondolas and slow-paced riders will enjoy the stationary ones.
FastPass: None

★ **Magic Tips** ★

1. The top makes for some amazing photos of the resort.
2. The line for this ride can be very long and slow paced. Unfortunately, because there is no FastPass or Single Rider Line, we've yet to discover a faster way to ride this attraction. It's recommended to ride at the start of the day after you get your FastPass for another attraction.
2. This ride may close in the early evening due to its use in the World of Color.
3. You can control the colors on the Fun Wheel at night by playing the "California Adventure Fun Wheel Challenge" just before the World of Color show (see World of Color description for game details)
4. If you get motion sickness easily, we don't recommend the swinging gondolas

Golden Zephyr

Description: Whirl in a giant, slow-paced circle on a metallic aircraft.
Level: Young Kids / Family
Recommendation: Perfect for young kids and those who enjoy slow rides.
FastPass: None

Silly Symphony Swings

Description: Classic spinning carnival swings that fly around to orchestral music.

Level: Everyone (must be 40"/ 102cm or taller)

Recommendation: Everyone from kids to thrill riders will love this whirl of a ride.

FastPass: None

Note: *Tandem swings available*

Goofy's Sky School

Description: A twisting family-friendly rollercoaster.

Level: Kids / Thrill riders (must be 42"/ 1027m or taller)

Recommendation: perfect for Thrill riders of all ages

FastPass: Available

★ **Magic Tips** ★

1. Check the FastPass return time for Goofy's Sky School. Often, it's only an hour or so after the time you get the pass.
2. The seats can be a bit uncomfortable for larger riders.

Jumpin' Jellyfish

Description: Bob up and down on these jellyfish-shaped parachute seats.

Level: Young Kids / Kids

Recommendation: Perfect for kids of all ages

FastPass: None

Shows and Attractions

World of Color

Description: A stunning nighttime water show that takes guests through several Disney films and dazzling technical effects!

Thrill Level: Everyone / Family
Recommendation: Must see for all
FastPass: Available. We recommend getting to the park at opening to guarantee a reserved spot as FastPass selections run out quickly. Getting a World of Color FastPass will not affect you getting another FastPass right after.

Get Preferred Viewing with Dinner Packages - Reserve a World of Color 3-course meal package to receive a voucher to the preferred viewing areas:

1. Book at Ariel's Grotto (our top recommendation), Carthay Circle Restaurant, or Wine Country Trattoria for the voucher.
2. Dessert Package ($79 per person) - choose from several different desserts and receive a sparkling beverage while you watch the show.
3. Book, visit Disneyland.com or call (714) 781-4565

★ **Magic Tips** ★

To get the best view, start at Disney California Adventure when the park opens and reserve your FastPass. These often run out early, so make sure you reserve yours.

Note: *Getting a FastPass to World of Color will not affect you getting any other passes throughout the day.*
If you don't get reserved seating, there is only limited standing room, so make sure you get to your spot well ahead of time (we recommend at least 45 minutes before the start of the show).

Be Part of the Lighting Magic

- Get a "Made with Magic" Mickey or Minnie Mouse hat that light up with the show (Mickey Gloves light as well). These can be purchased at the park stores for $20-$30. They can also be purchased at the Main Street shops in Disneyland or Off the Page in Hollywood Land.

• Want to control the color? You can by playing a special online game with your mobile device. Connect to the "PierGames" Wi-Fi on your device (up to 45 minutes from show time) for the game to pop up in your browser. Use your memory skills to compete against others in the park. The winner will be able to control the colors of Mickey's Fun Wheel for 30 seconds!

Control the Colors on Mickey's Fun Wheel

A game that appears before the World of Color show begins.

1. 45 minutes before the start of the show, log your mobile device onto the Wi-Fi network, "PierGames".
2. Open your browser to play the game (no app download needed)
3. Play a color memory game against others in the park. The winner controls the colors of the Fun Wheel for 30 seconds!

Pacific Wharf

Theme: A San Francisco-style dock packed with restaurants.

★ Magic Tips ★

There is plenty of seating here though we recommend going outside of the lunch and dinner times to avoid the crowds.

1. Lunch before 11.30am or after 2.30pm.
2. Dinner before 4.30pm or after 7:30pm.

Shows and Attractions

The Bakery Tour
Description: Take a tour of the Boudin Bakery at Disney California Adventure
Thrill Level: Everyone
Recommendation: Fun for bread-lovers
FastPass: None
★ **Magic Tip** ★ Get a free piece of sample bread on the tour!

Grizzly Peak

Theme: Californian national park-themed land. Get soaked on the Grizzly River Run or board the hang glider simulation, Soarin'!

★ **Magic Tip** ★ If you stay at the Grand Californian Hotel and Spa (or any other Disneyland Resort hotel), you can enter the park through an exclusive entrance that empties into Grizzly Peak via the Grand Californian Hotel.

Rides

Soarin'
Description: A hang glider simulation that takes you over stunning views, landmarks, and scents that fill the air.
Level: Everyone / Thrill Riders (must be 40"/ 102cm or taller)

Recommendation: A unique, must-see experience.
FastPass: Available
★ **Magic Tip** ★

1. Highly recommend getting a FastPass for this attraction as the line can get very long.
2. For the "Single Rider Line", ask a Cast Member at the FastPass entrance.
3. Guests can often line up for the popular Soarin' before the rest of the park opens! This is a great way to skip long lines that form later in the day, however, it may also hinder your chances of scoring a FastPass to some of the more popular rides like Radiator Springs Racers and Guardians of the Galaxy–Mission Breakout!

Grizzly River Run

Description: board a massive raft and travel up and down a gushing river.

Level: Everyone / Thrill Riders (must be 42"/ 107cm or taller)

Recommendation: Perfect for those who love water rides.

FastPass: Available

★ **Magic Tip** ★

1. The Single Rider Line is available by walking up the stairs to the exit of the ride just before the rotating platform.
2. Even when the line is long for this ride, you can sometimes score a FastPass only an hour away. If you have availability, make sure that you use it!
3. On colder days, however, a FastPass is often not needed as Grizzly River Run typically doesn't have a very long lines during cooler weather.

Redwood Creek Challenge Trail

Description: Inspired by the Pixar movie, *Up* and Disney's *Brother Bear*, kids can earn Wilderness Explorer badges by completing challenges.

Level: Kids / Family

Recommendation: A playground for kids of all ages.

FastPass: None

CHAPTER ELEVEN
DOWNTOWN DISNEY

Introduction

Downtown Disney is the premier hangout location at the Disneyland Resort. It's surrounded by the resort hotels, bursting with shops including World of Disney, and filled with treats like an enormous Starbucks and tasty Jamba Juice. Also catch the latest blockbusters at the AMC Theatre, go for a round of bowling at Splitsville, or play arcade games and watch live sports games at the ESPN Zone. Best of all, theme park admission isn't required to experience the fun of Downtown Disney.

Monorail - Save your feet from walking and take Walt Disney's monorail system into Disneyland's Tomorrowland station. The ride comes with some great narration and tips about the park. You must have a park ticket to board.

Dress Code: No need to dress up! Come in your Disneyland-approved theme park clothing.
Note: *We cover Downtown Disney's many delicious restaurants in the next chapter.*

Shops

Disney-Themed Shops

World of Disney® - This ultimate Disney store is massive and located close to the parks

Anna & Elsa's Boutique - Disney collectables and apparel

Disney Vault 28 - Unique Disney collectables

Disney's Pin Traders - A place to buy Disney pins

D-Street - Hip Disney apparel and collectables

Mall Shops

Quiksilver® - Beach-inspired apparel and swimsuits

Fossil® - Leather apparel and accessories

Sanuk® - Shoes and sandals

Something Silver® - Jewelry and accessories

Sunglass Icon® - Sunglasses and accessories

Sephora® - Makeup and beauty supplies

Rainforest Café® Retail Shopping Village - Collectables and apparel

More Fun

The LEGO® Store - Purchase and play with building blocks. Also check out the enormous Disney characters made entirely of Legos!

WonderGround Gallery - Disney Art for viewing and for sale.

Marceline's Confectionery - Pick through a wide assortment of candy and gifts.

AMC Theatre 12 - Grab some popcorn and see a movie located near the Disneyland Hotel. www.amctheatres.com

Splitsville - Bowl, drink, and dine at this premier alley (opens early 2018)

Stages - During the day and at night, Downtown Disney comes alive with live music

Hotel Restaurants - Visit one of the 3 resort hotels and dine at one of their restaurants, stop at a bar, or recline in a lounge.

Coming Soon

Star Wars: Secrets of the Empire - A unique, groundbreaking "hyper-reality" attraction is coming to Downtown Disney. A family-friendly virtual reality gaming experience created by THE VOID in collaboration with LucasFilm and ILMxLab. Opening date has not been announced, though we expect either late 2018 or early 2019.

CHAPTER TWELVE

DINING GUIDE

Introduction

Many visitors to the Disneyland Resort tell us that mostly they come for the world-class rides and meeting their favorite Disney characters. Sometimes they'll mention a particular show like the nighttime fireworks or Fantasmic, but rarely do they mention one of our favorite attractions: the food!

If you haven't already thought about the dining at Disney, we recommend that you start now. The resort holds a wide variety of famous mouthwatering treats and even better little-known delights! Sometimes we visit the resort just to try our favorite snacks and sneak a ride or two in between munchies–we're not kidding! In this chapter we review all of the Disneyland's dining experiences and place *"Top Choice!"* next to our favorites or a "★" by our secondary recommendations.

Disneyland Dining

Main Street, U.S.A.

The Carnation Café
Description: Early 20th-century American café with classic.
Type: Table-service
Age Group: Everyone
Pricing: $$
Try This: The breakfast here is quite good with Mickey-shaped waffles. If you enjoy coffee, we recommend ordering a cup with the Mickey Mouse souvenir mug. For lunch, the Main Street Cheeseburger, Sourdough Bacon-Cheese Melt, and Green Chili Burger are delicious. The Carnation Café also has amazing malts.

Market House (Starbucks)
Description: Yep, even Disneyland has a Starbucks!
Type: Coffee Shop
Age Group: Adults
Pricing: $
Try This: The lines can be somewhat long in the morning, but they are quick to service everyone.
Tip: It might be a little hard to find the Market House sign, but it is right across from the Carnation Café, on your right as you walk toward the castle.

Plaza Inn
Description: A classic, wonderfully detailed restaurant on the corner of Main Street and Tomorrowland.
Type: Table-service with character buffet
Age Group: Everyone
Pricing: $$

Try This: The fried chicken is famous here. You can also have breakfast with Minnie and her friends.

Inexpensive Eats

Gibson Girl Ice Cream Parlor - Serving up Disneyland's scrumptious ice cream. Get it in a waffle cone.
Refreshment Corner - Get a Coke soft drink or, better yet, a famous chili dog here.
Jolly Holiday Bakery Café - *Mary Poppins*-themed fresh bakery with delicious treats, coffee, and tea.

Adventureland

⋆ **Bengal Barbecue**
Description: South Asian style barbecue serving coffee drinks, soda pops, and delicious kabobs.
Type: Fast service
Age Group: Adults (no kids' menu)
Price: $$
Try This: The Bengal Beef Skewer or the Outback Vegetable Skewer.

★ **Tiki Juice Bar (hosted by Dole)** - *Top Choice!*
Description: Juice bar serving the famous Disneyland Dole Whip.
Type: Fast Service stand
Age Group: Everyone
Price: $
Try This: the pineapple-flavored Dole Whip floats are one of Disneyland's most famous recipes and our top treat recommendation.
★ **Magic Tip** ★ The line may be long, but it's worth it. However, in the summer, we've seen the line nearly an hour during the hottest parts of the day. It may be wise to come back when the day has cooled along with the line.

Frontierland

The Golden Horseshoe
Description: Western dining experience with American fare
Type: Fast service
Age Group: Everyone
Price: $$
Try This: Chili in a Bread Bowl

River Belle Terrace
Description: western dining experience with American fare
Type: Fast service
Age Group: Everyone
Price: $$
Try This: Pork Spareribs or River Belle's Chopped Salad

Stage Door Café
Description: Western dining experience with American favorites
Age Group: Everyone
Type: Fast service
Price: $
Try This: Hand-dipped corn dog

Rancho del Zocalo Restaurante
Description: Mexican food
Type: Fast service
Age Group: Everyone
Price: $$
Try This: Mickey Mouse Pancake for Breakfast or Citrus Fire-grilled Chicken or Burrito Guadalajara for lunch/dinner.
★ **Magic Tips** ★
The pumpkin flan during Halloween (mid-September - October) and Tres Leche Cake at the Holiday time (November - December) are fan favorite desserts!

New Orleans Square

★ **Blue Bayou Restaurant** - *Top Choice!*
Description: Disneyland's premier dining experience with some of the best entrees the Disneyland Resort has to offer. Located inside of the Pirates of the Caribbean ride, this is exceptional Louisiana-style dining with creole food and more. Even in the middle of the day, you will feel as though you are dining next to a Louisiana Bayou at night!
Type: Table service
Age Group: Everyone
Price: $$$$

Try This:

1. *Le Special de* Monte Cristo Sandwich is our absolute favorite entrée in the entire resort!
    - **a.** The Monte Cristo is a battered and fried sandwich filled with ham, turkey, and Swiss cheese. To top it off, there are dipping sauces (berry jam and a sweet crème), plus the sandwich is dusted with powder sugar. We know it sounds odd to newbies, but it's an absolute delight and worth trying!
    - **b.** This is a lot of food for most people (the large sandwich comes in four pieces). You can always split the entrée to save money as the meal also comes with a side salad and fruit skewer.
    - **c.** The Monte Cristo is *only* served at lunch and sometimes only by special order, so ask the host if you don't see it listed on the outside menu
2. Gumbo - A delicious soup packed with blends of Cajun seasoning served in a small cup with rice. Gumbo comes as an option with most entrees and we highly recommend it!

★ **Magic Tips** ★

1. Book your reservation EARLY for the Blue Bayou on Disneyland.com (or call 714-781-DINE). You can book up to 60 days in advance.
2. If you can't get a reservation at all, check Café Orleans as they tend have more availability and a similar menu with outdoor seating.

★ **Café Orleans**

Description: French-style soups, sandwiches, crepes, and salads in the center of New Orleans Square. This is a great alternative to the Blue Bayou with outdoor seating and views of the Rivers of America.

Type: Table service

Age Group: Everyone

Price: $$$

Try This: Monte Cristo Sandwich (see Blue Bayou description above), Three-Cheese Monte Cristo, New Orleans Gumbo, or Chicken Gumbo Crepe.

★ **Magic Tip** ★

> We also recommend booking in advance at Disneyland.com (or call 714-781-DINE). You can book up to 60 days in advance.

French Market Restaurant

Description: French-style soups, sandwiches, crepes, and salads in the center of New Orleans Square. This is a great alternative to the Blue Bayou with outdoor seating and views of the Rivers of America.

Type: Fast Service

Age Group: Everyone

Price: $$

Try This: French Dip Sandwich or Creamy Corn Chowder (served in a bread bowl)

Royal Street Veranda

Description: French-style soups

Type: Fast service

Age Group: Adults and Teenagers

Price: $$

Try This: Creamy Clam Chowder (served in a sourdough bread bowl).

Inexpensive Eats

Mint Julep Bar ($) - Mickey-shaped beignets, lattes, mochas, and, of course, mint juleps.

//

Critter Country

⋆ **Harbour Galley**
Description: Waterfront-style food with lobster entrées
Type: Fast service
Age Group: Everyone
Price: $
Try This: Lobster Bisque or Lobster Roll

⋆ **Hungry Bear Restaurant**
Description: Picnic-style sandwiches, burgers, and fries
Type: Fast service
Age Group: Everyone (many kids' choices)
Price: $
Try This: Turkey Caesar Wrap and Onion Rings, or a burger
⋆ **Magic Tips** ⋆

1. There is quieter seating here by the Rivers of America. After ordering your food, walk to the back of the upstairs patio and all of the way to the back by the water.
2. If you miss the Country Bear Jamboree, remnants of the original show can be seen around the restaurant.

//

Fantasyland

★ **Red Rose Taverne (Village Haus Restaurant)**
Description: French and American-fusion restaurant styled after *Beauty and the Beast* (2017)
Type: Fast service
Age Group: Everyone
Price: $$
Try This: Chicken Sandwich a la Lumiere (lunch or dinner), Grey Stuff Gateau (for dessert), and Gaston's Famous Brew to drink
Note: *This also was the location of the Village Haus Restaurant. Disney hasn't confirmed it, but this location may chance back to Village Haus, which is a European and American-fusion restaurant.*

Troubadour Tavern
Description: Italian, German, and American-fusion restaurant
Type: Fast service snacks
Age Group: Everyone
Price: $$
Try This: Bacon and Sour Cream Stuffed Baked Potato.

Inexpensive Eats

Maurice's Treats
Description: European-style pastries served from a cart inspired by *Beauty and the Beast*.
Try This: Strawberry Twist and the Boysen Apple Freeze

Mickey's Toontown

Inexpensive Eats

Daisy's Diner - The personal-sized pizzas are tasty

Pluto's Dog House - Scrumptious hot dogs

Clarabelle's - We recommend the Mickey Ice Cream Sandwich

//

Tomorrowland

Galactic Grill
Description: American-style breakfast, lunch, and dinner
Type: Fast service
Age Group: Everyone (many kids' options)
Price: $$
Try This: We find Galactic Grill's food to be a bit unsatisfying with bland breakfast burritos and burgers
Note: *Galaxy Grill also offers late-night dining*

Redd Rocket's Pizza Port
Description: Pizza, pasta, salads, and desserts
Type: Cafeteria Style
Age Group: Everyone (many kids' options)
Price: $$
Try This: Mega Pepperoni slice and a Side Salad
Note: *The bread sticks look good, but they are fairly bland.*

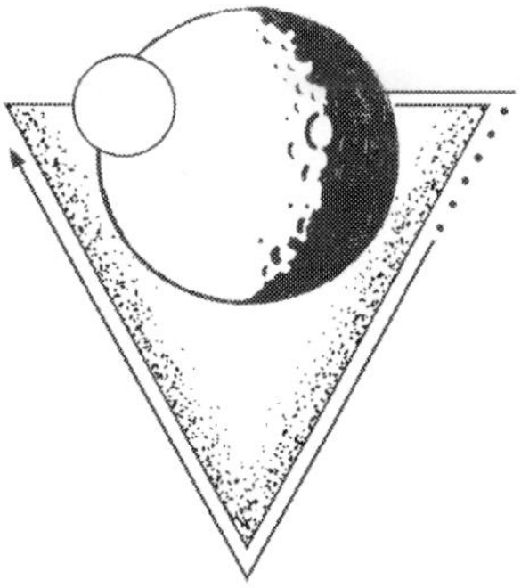

<u>Tomorrowland Skyline Lounge Experience</u>

Description: Snack, sip, and savor a delicious view of the Disneyland nighttime fireworks from a high-up lounge in Tomorrowland!

Type: Special Event Dining

Age Group: Everyone

Price: $45 / person

Try This: If you're craving a great view of the fireworks, but also want to relax at night in a posh setting, this experience is for you! Of course, it does come at an extra premium cost ($45 per person), but you'll have a wonderful, full view of the castle and the show while snacking on a tray of fruit, cheese, and sweets. There is also a selection of hot or cold beverages (usually sodas and coffee, but no alcohol). The lounge is pretty cool, too, with futuristic light-up tables and swanky seating positioned at the top of the Tomorrowland Expo Center (once the Innoventions building, but now houses Star Wars Launch Bay).

⋆ **Magic Tip** ⋆

We highly recommend booking early or you may miss out on this experience (up to 60 days in advance). Reserve Your Table **https://disneyland.disney.go.com/dining/disneyland/tomorrowland-skyline-lounge**

California Adventure Dining

Buena Vista Street

Carthay Circle Restaurant

Description: Disney California Adventure's signature dining location with some of the best entrees the Disneyland Resort has to offer

Type: Table Service with adult beverages available

Age Group: Adults and Teens (kids' meals available)

Price: $$$$

Try This:

Starter: Carthay Signature Fried Biscuits - flakey pastries with an unforgettable blend of bacon, white cheddar, and jalapeno. Served with sweet apricot honey butter.

Entrée: all of the food here is delicious, but we recommend the Crispy Maple Leaf Duck Confit Salad for lunch or the Artichoke Crepes for dinner.

Dessert: Warm Dulce de Leche Marshmallow Turnover.

★ **Magic Tips** ★

1. Carthay Circle has a fancy atmosphere, but no need to dress up. The Disneyland Resort expects to see the guests in their normal park attire.
2. We highly recommend booking a reservation before visiting the park at Disneyland.com (or call 714-781-DINE). You can book up to 60 days in advance.
3. If you can't get a reservation and the line is too long, Carthay Circle Lounge is a similar second option.

<u>Carthay Circle Lounge</u>
Description: A snacks and bites lounge that many adults will enjoy. Serves sushi and alcohol drinks.
Type: Adult beverages and finger foods
Age Group: Adult
Price: $$$
Try This: Tostaditas with Mole Verde-braised Pork Cheeks -A Mexican entrée with queso and avocado.

<u>Fiddler, Fifer, and Practical Café</u> (serves Starbucks Coffee)
Description: Coffee shop
Type: Fast Service
Age Group: Everyone
Price: $
Try This: Spinach, Feta, and Cage-Free Egg White (breakfast wrap)

<u>Fairfax Market</u>
Description: A place to purchase healthy snacks and vegetarian options.
Type: "On-the-Go"
Age Group: Everyone
Price: $
Try This: Hummus to snack, coconut water to drink.

Inexpensive Eats

Clarabelle's Hand Scooped Ice Cream ($) - We recommend the Oswald Sundae (also available in a souvenir holder shaped like a kitchen sink)

Mortimer's Fish Market ($) - A great place to pick up snacks and bottled water.

//

Hollywood Land

★ **Schmoozies**
Description: Blended fruit drinks
Type: Fast Service snacks
Age Group: Everyone
Price: $
Try This: The Dynamic Duo - blend of pineapple and strawberries with low-fat yogurt.

★ **Award Wieners** - *Top Choice!*
Description: Gourmet hot dogs and sausages
Type: Fast service
Age Group: Everyone
Price: $
Try This: Sicilian Sausage - Tastes like a delicious sausage pizza.

Studio Catering Co.
Description: Non-alcoholic drinks
Type: Fast Service snacks
Age Group: Everyone
Price: $
Try This: Wonderland Watermelon Frozen Lemonade - a delicious slushy that you can also get in an Alice in Wonderland souvenir cup.

Inexpensive Eats

Fairfax Market ($) - A place to purchase "On-the-Go" healthy snacks and vegetarian options.

Cars Land

Flo's V8 Café
Description: Classic American Diner
Type: Fast Service
Age Group: Everyone
Price: $$
Try This:

1. Breakfast - American Breakfast (bacon, eggs, potatoes, and a biscuit).
2. Lunch & Dinner - BBQ Pork Ribs (comes with Coca-Cola™ BBQ sauce and mashed potatoes).

★ **Cozy Cone Motel**
Description: Cone-shaped food booths that serve delicious snacks.
Type: Fast Service Snacks
Age Group: Everyone
Price: $
Try This: Churro (ask for the caramel sauce) and the Chili Cone Queso (beef or vegetarian chili with cheddar cheese and corn chips served in a bread bowl).

Inexpensive Eats

Fillmore's Taste-In ($): Fast Service snacks, juice, and water.

a bug's land

Inexpensive Eats

Churro Cart: Also serves Coca-Cola drinks

//

Pacific Wharf

Alfresco Tasting Terrace
Description: Wines and bar snacks with a park view on the terrace
Type: Bar and Lounge
Age Group: Adults
Price: $$ - $$$$ (depending on the wine)
Try This:

1. Try a Disney Family Wine (21 and older)
2. Charcuterie Cheese Board (delectable prosciutto, chorizo, blue cheese, olives, walnuts, and more)

Cocina Cucamonga Mexican Grill ($$) - We recommend the Burrito Sonora with Beef (cheese and beef burritos served with refried beans and rice).

Lucky Fortune Cookery ($$) - Chinese food, we recommend an Asian Rice Bowl with chicken (similar to orange chicken served on steamed white rice).

Pacific Wharf Café ($$) - Made with the deliciously famous Boudin bread, we recommend the clam chowder or broccoli and cheese soup in a sourdough bread bowl.

Wine Country Trattoria ($$) - Try the Red Sangria (21 and older) and the Bolognese.

Adult Pours

Pacific Wharf Distribution Co. ($) - Popular beer on tap for adults (21 and older).

⋆ **Rita's Baja Blenders** ($)- *Top Choice!* - For a double shot of tequila, ask for the Grand Margarita (21 and older).

Sonoma Terrace ($) - Try a Local California Craft Beer (21 and older).

Mendocino Terrace ($$) - Wines (for 21 and older) and soft drinks. We recommend pairing wine with the Italian Meat and Cheese Box

Inexpensive Eats

Ghirardelli Soda Fountain and Chocolate Shop ($) - Browse delicious chocolate gift or order a creamy soda. Also get a free chocolate sample when you enter!

Paradise Pier

Ariel's Grotto

Description: American dining

Type: Table Service (Character dining also available for breakfast and lunch)

Age Group: Everyone (especially families with kids)

Price: $$$$

Try This:

Breakfast - All-American Breakfast (hickory-smoked bacon or sausage, scrambled eggs, hash browns, and oats)

Lunch - Red Oaked-Smoked Honey-Whisky Barbecue Tri-Tip (served with mashed potatoes and vegetables)

Dinner - Grilled Lobster Tail and Red Oaked-Smoked Honey-Whisky Barbecue Tri Tip (served with mashed potatoes and vegetables)

Cocktails - Magical Star Cocktail (passion fruit blend with coconut rum served over a glowing ice cube that you can keep) or Moscow Mule (vodka with ginger beer, lime, and agave nectar)

★ **Magic Tips** ★

1. Book in advance to avoid lines (Disneyland.com or call 714-781-DINE)
2. You can also get reserved seating for World of Color by booking your dinner reservation early.

★ **Cove Bar** - *Top Choice!*

Description: Disney California Adventure's popular bar with a view of the water and Paradise Pier.

Type: Casual Table Service and Bar

Age Group: Adults and Teens (there are tasty non-alcoholic options for nondrinkers)
Price: $$
Try This:

1. CB Lobster Nachos - Zesty nachos supreme (tortilla chips, black beans, cheese blend, and chipotle crème) with many flavorful bits of lobster.
2. Trio of Tri-Tip Sliders - Made with bacon, arugula, and blue cheese.
3. Cocktails - Habanero Lime Margarita (Patron tequila, habanero lime, and sweet-and-sour) or Moscow Mule (vodka with ginger beer, lime, and agave nectar)
4. Non-Alcoholic Drink - Wild Strawberry Lemonade

★ **Magic Tip** ★ get to the bar before 11:30am to avoid the lines that begin around that time (even a short line can take an hour or more for seating).

★ **Paradise Garden Grill**
Description: A California-style grill.
Age Group: Everyone
Price: $$
Try This: Grilled Steak Skewer (served with rice, cucumber salad, and pita bread).

Adult Pours

Bayside Brews
Description: Popular beer on tap for adults (21 and older)
Age Group: Adult
Price: $
Try This: Many standard choices so we recommend picking your favorite brand.

Inexpensive Eats

★ **Corn Dog Castle**
Description: get a delicious, battered hot dog with Disney's famous recipe.

Paradise Pier Ice Cream Company
Description: Come here your favorite flavor of soft-serve ice cream (or a root beer float)

Grizzly Peak

Smokejumpers Grill
Description: A hanger-shaped American grill for burger and fries
Type: Fast Service
Age Group: Everyone
Price: $$
Try This: Bacon Cheddar Burger and Chili-Cheese Fries

Inexpensive Eats

Refreshment Point ($) - Coca Cola beverages

Resort Hotel Dining

Disneyland Hotel

★ **Goofy's Kitchen** - *Top Choice!*
Description: American Breakfast and Dinner with buffet options.
Type: Table Service (Breakfast and Dinner)
Age Group: Everyone
Price: $$$$
Adult Beverages: Yes
Reservations: Disneyland.com or (714) 781-3463
Try This: Breakfast or Dinner buffets

Steakhouse 55
Description: Elegant American Steakhouse
Type: Table Service (Breakfast and Dinner)
Age Group: Everyone
Price: $$$$
Adult Beverages: Yes
Reservations: Disneyland.com or (714) 781-3463
Try This:

Starter: Maryland Crab Cake
Entrée: the steaks here are delicious!

Tangaroa Terrace
Description: American and Polynesian Cuisine
Type: Fast Service (Breakfast, Lunch, and Dinner)
Price: $$
Age Group: Everyone
Adult Beverages: Yes
Reservations: Disneyland.com or (714) 781-3463

Try This:

Breakfast: French Toast (with banana-caramel sauce)
Lunch or Dinner: Angus Hawaiian Cheeseburger

Bars and Lounges

★ **Trader Sam's Enchanted Tiki Bar** - *Top Choice!*

Description: located by the Disneyland Hotel Pool, this authentic Disney "dive bar" serves American food with a full bar. Volcanos erupt and storms brew inside of the room with the order of certain drinks. We never thought that Disneyland would make a dive bar, but we are so glad that they did! Trader Sam's is fun for everyone (though it becomes 21 and over after 8pm).

Type: "Dive Bar" and Lounge

Age Group: Adult (though there are options for kids)

Price: $$

Adult Beverages: Yes (full bar and cocktails)

Reservations: None

Try This:

Cocktails: The Uh Oa! (rum blends with passion fruit), Krakatoa Punch (rum punch), and Ka-blue-ie! (tropical rum with blue curacao) are our personal favorites.
Eats: The Angus Hawaiian Cheeseburger or Chicken Lettuce Wraps.

★ **Magic Tips** ★

1. "Adult Dole Whip" - this is a secret menu item for those who love the tropical-flavored drinks. The concoction is made with rum, pineapple juice, and some other things we can't place. It's recommended that you sit at the bar and get friendly with a bartender to ask for the drink. Not every bartender there will know how to make it.

2. Trader Sam's doesn't list their drink prices, but they are often anywhere from $10 - $30 (the higher priced drinks are the ones that make the room erupt or storm).

The Lounge at Steakhouse 55
Description: The bar at Steakhouse 55 restaurant
Type: Elegant Bar and Lounge
Age Group: Adult
Price: $$
Adult Beverages: Yes (full bar and cocktails)
Reservations: None
Try This:

Cocktails: Any! They are all fantastic choices.
Eats: Main Lobster Roll Sliders.

//

Disney Grand Californian

⋆ **Storytellers Café** - *Top Choice!*
Description: American Breakfast, Lunch, and Dinner with buffet options.
Type: Table Service (and Character Breakfast)
Age Group: Everyone
Price: Breakfast and Dinner $$$$ (Lunch $$$)
Adult Beverages: Yes (Lunch and Dinner)
Reservations: Disneyland.com or (714) 781-3463
Try This:

Breakfast: Brunch Buffet
Lunch: Slow-roasted Turkey Clubhouse
Dinner: Dinner Buffet

Napa Rose

Description: California-themed Upscale Dining with entrées designed by gourmet Napa chef, Andrew Sutton.

Type: Dinner

Age Group: Adult (though there are options for kids)

Price: $$$$

Adult Beverages: Yes (great wine selection)

Reservations: Disneyland.com or (714) 781-3463

Try This:

Starter: Roasted Breast of Pheasant with Duck Liver Mousseline

Lunch: Any of the main courses as they were all designed by gourmet Chef Andrew Sutton.

Dinner: Dinner Buffet

Bars and Lounges

Napa Rose Lounge
Description: The bar lounge inside of the Napa Rose (more casual than Napa Rose).
Type: Lounge
Age Group: Adult
Price: $$
Adult Beverages: Yes (full bar, wine, and cocktails)
Reservations: None
Try This:

Wine: Domaine Chandon, Etoile, Brut Rose (Californian Sparkling Rose)

Cocktails: Moscow Mule (vodka, lime, ginger beer in a copper mug)

Eats: The wood-fired Pizzetta of the Season or Wine County Pheasant Meatloaf

Hearthstone Lounge
Description: a bar lounge
Type: Lounge (lobby)
Price: $$
Age Group: Adult
Adult Beverages: Yes (wine, beer, and cocktails)
Reservations: None
Try This:

Wine and Cocktails: see "Napa Rose Lounge

Eats: Two Mini Wagyu Sliders (served with skinny fries)

Disney Paradise Pier Hotel

Disney's PCH Grill -*Great Choice!*
Description: American Buffet Breakfast and Dinner with Buffet Options.
Type: Table Service (and Character Breakfast)
Age Group: Everyone
Price: Breakfast and Dinner $$$
Adult Beverages: None
Reservations: Disneyland.com or (714) 781-3463
Try This: Breakfast or Dinner Buffet

Bars and Lounges

Surfside Lounge
Description: California beach-themed bar and lounge
Type: Lounge (Breakfast snacks, full lunch and dinner)
Age Group: Everyone
Price: $$
Adult Beverages: Yes (full bar, wine, and cocktails)
Reservations: None
Try This:

Breakfast: "Mickey" Waffles
Appetizer: beer-battered Onion Rings or Monterey Bay Spinach and Artichoke Dip
Lunch/Dinner: Paradise Pier Club (turkey club)

The Sand Bar
Description: California beach-themed bar near the lobby
Type: Lounge (drinks and sandwiches)
Age Group: Adult
Price: $$
Adult Beverages: Yes (full bar, wine, and cocktails)
Reservations: None

Downtown Disney Dining

Table Service Restaurants

⋆ **Catal Restaurant** - *Top Choice!*
Description: American and Mediterranean entrées
Type: Table Service
Age Group: Everyone
Price: $$$
Adult Beverages: Yes
Reservations: Disneyland.com or (714) 781-3463
Try This:
Starter: Crispy Calamari
Entrée: Crispy Suckling Pig (pork and roasted Brussel sprouts) or the Marinated Angus Hangar Steak (served with mashed potatoes)

⋆ **ESPN Zone**
Description: American sports-themed restaurant and bar. The upstairs section has sports-themed arcade games.
Type: Table Service / Lounge
Age Group: Everyone
Price: $$ - $$$
Adult Beverages: Yes (full bar with beer on tap)
Try This: Smokehouse Burger (savory bacon, cheddar, and barbecue sauce burger service with fries or a salad)

La Brea Bakery Café
Description: Brunch and dinner menus
Type: Casual Service
Age Group: Everyone

Price: $$
Adult Beverages: Yes
Try This: Margherita Pizza
Note: *Get Fast Service sandwiches at the La Brea Bakery Express next door.*

Rainforest Café

Description: Dine in a rainforest filled with lush plants, waterfalls, and animatronics that come to life when the occasional storms brews in the restaurant! Perfect for families with kids though fine-diners may want to skip this one.
Type: Table Service
Age Group: Family (kids will especially love this place)
Price: $$
Adult Beverages: Yes (Wine and Beer)
Reservations: Disneyland.com or (714) 772-0413
Try This: Get a seat next to the aquarium.

Naples Ristorante e Pizzeria

Description: Italian
Type: Table Service
Age Group: Everyone
Price: $$$
Adult Beverages: Yes
Try This: get your favorite type of pizza

Ralph Brennan's Jazz Kitchen

Description: Cajun food with a lounge bar
Type: Table Service / Lounge
Age Group: Adults and teenagers (though they have options for kids)
Price: $$
Adult Beverages: Yes
Reservations: Disneyland.com or (714) 781-3463

Try This: Fried Chicken Po-Boy or Creole Chicken Caesar Wrap

Note: *For fast service sandwiches, visit the Jazz Kitchen Express next door.*

⋆ **Splitsville** (Coming late 2017/early 2018)

Description: Bowling and dining

Type: Upscale Bowling Alley Lounge

Age Group: All Ages

Price: $$

Adult Beverages: Yes

Reservations: Disneyland.com or (714) 781-3463

Note: *Splitsville is known for its great dining choices! Don't expect the typical bowling alley dining here, but a great menu with lots of American favorites for all!*

Tortilla Jo's

Description: Mexican food with a lounge bar

Type: Table Service / Lounge

Age Group: Everyone

Price: $$

Adult Beverages: Yes

Reservations: Disneyland.com or (714) 781-3463

Try This:

- Fajita de Tres (sizzling chicken, steak, and shrimp served with corns tortillas, rice, and beans)
- Shredded Beef Burrito (served with rice and refried beans) or the TJ's Grilled Chicken Caesar Salad

Note: *For Fast service Mexican food, visit the Taqueria next door.*

Casual Dining

Earl of Sandwich - *Top Choice!*
Description: American Sandwiches
Type: Fast Service
Age Group: Everyone
Price: $
Adult Beverages: Yes (Beer and Wine)
Try This: The Earl Club (turkey, bacon, Swiss cheese hot sandwich)

Napolini
Description: Pizza by the slice
Age Group: Everyone
Type: Table Service
Price: $$
Adult Beverages: No
Try This: get your favorite type of pizza

Bars, Lounges, and Inexpensive Eats

Uva Bar ($$) - A trendy outdoor bar with breakfast, lunch, and dinner options.

Starbucks® ($) - Coffee, pastries, and breakfast sandwiches

Jamba Juice ($) - Blended fruit smoothies

Haagen-Dazs® ($) - Ice cream

Wetzel's Pretzels ($) - Savory and sweet pretzels

CHAPTER THIRTEEN
CHARACTER LOCATIONS

Introduction

You can meet most of your favourite Disney, Marvel, Pixar, and Star Wars characters at the resort. They are always happy to sign autographs, interact, and take a photo with you. Disneyland is home to all of the classics from Mickey and Minnie to Donald and Daisy. But it doesn't stop there! Princesses roam Fantasyland while Stormtroopers from *Star Wars* stomp the Tomorrowland grounds. In Disney California Adventure's Hollywood Land, you can even meet Marvel's Spider-man and Captain America. Aren't sure if you should meet a character? We recommend it! After greeting Mickey, Chewbacca, or a Disney Princess, even an adult will have a smile that won't go away!

Hacks for Easily Finding Characters

1. Download the Disneyland App on your mobile device to track the characters!
2. Many of them have "show times" in certain locations. Be sure to check the character times on your resort map before visiting.
3. Character dining in the Disneyland Hotels and in the theme parks have many characters who will interact with you while you eat.
4. You may also see them walking around the parks or in the shows and parades.

Note: *Sadly, not every character comes out each day. However, one of your favorites is sure to be there!*

Character Locations (alphabetical)

Aladdin - Aladdin's Oasis (Adventureland)
Anna - Animation Academy (Disney California Adventure)
Ariel - Ariel's Grotto (Disney California Adventure)
Baloo - Adventureland (Disneyland)
Belle - Princess Fantasy Faire (Disneyland)
Black Widow - Hollywood Land (Disney California Adventure)
Boba Fett - Star Wars Launch Bay (Disneyland)
Buzz Lightyear - Tomorrowland (Disneyland)
Captain America - Hollywood Land (Disney California Adventure)
Chewbacca - Star Wars Launch Bay (Disneyland)
Chip 'n Dale - Chip 'n Dale Critter Breakfast at Storytellers Café (Disney's Grand Californian Hotel)
Cruella de Ville - Hollywood Land (Disney California Adventure)
Crush the Turtle - *Turtle Talk with Crush* at Disney Animation (Disney Hollywood Studios)
Daisy Duck - Toon Town (Disneyland)
Donald Duck - Donald's Boat in Toon Town (Disneyland)
Duffy the Bear - Paradise Pier (Disneyland)
Darth Vader - Jedi Training / Star Wars Launch Bay (Disneyland)
Eeyore - Critter Country (Disneyland)
Elsa - Animation Academy (Disney California Adventure)
Elastigirl (Pixar's *The Incredibles*) - Hollywood Land (Disney California Adventure)
Flik (Pixar's *A Bug's Life*) - "a bug's land" (Disney California Adventure)
Frollo (*The Hunchback of Notre Dame*) - Halloween Time (Disneyland, mid-September - October 31st)

Frozone (The Incredibles) - Hollywood land (Disney California Adventure)

Gamora - Hollywood Land (Disney California Adventure)

Goofy - Goofy's Playhouse in Toon Town (Disneyland)

Groot (Adult) - Hollywood Land (Disney California Adventure)

Handy Manny - Hollywood Land (Disney California Adventure)

Jack Sparrow - New Orleans Square (Disneyland)

Jack Skellington - Holiday time in front of the Haunted Mansion (Disneyland, September - December)

Kylo Ren - Star Wars Launch Bay (Disneyland)

Princess Jasmine - Aladdin's Oasis (Disneyland)

Lightning McQueen - see him driving around Cars Land (Disney California Adventure)

Mad Hatter - Fantasyland (Disneyland)

Mary Poppins - Fantasyland (Disneyland)

Mater - Cars Land (Disney California Adventure)

Meeko (*Pocahontas*) - Character Breakfast at the Storytellers Café (Disney's Grand Californian Hotel)

Mickey Mouse - at his home in Toon Town (Disneyland)

Minnie Mouse - at her home in Toon Town (Disneyland)

Mr. Potato Head - interact with him in the queue for Toy Story Midway Mania™ (Disney California Adventure)

Oswald the Lucky Rabbit - Buena Vista Street (Disney California Adventure)

Peter Pan - Fantasyland (Disneyland)

Piglet - Critter Country (Disneyland)

Pluto - Toon Town (Disneyland)

Prince Phillip - Fantasyland (Disneyland)

Prince Naveen - New Orleans Square (Disneyland)

Queen of Hearts - Fantasyland (Disneyland) and Hollywood Land (Disney California Adventure)

Sally (The Nightmare Before Christmas) - Holiday time in front of the Haunted Mansion (Disneyland, September - December)

Sleeping Beauty - Princess Fantasy Faire (Disneyland)
Snow White - Main Street, U.S.A. or Princess Fantasy Faire (Disneyland)
Spider-man - Hollywood Land (Disney California Adventure)
Star Lord - Hollywood Land (Disney California Adventure)
Stormtroopers - Tomorrowland (Disneyland)
Sulley - Hollywood Land (Disney California Adventure)
Tiana - New Orleans Square (Disneyland)
Tigger - Critter Country (Disneyland)
Tinker Bell and her friends - Pixie Hallow (Disneyland)
Winnie the Pooh - Critter Country (Disneyland)

More Tips

• Kids will love the character autograph books sold on Main Street.
• During the holidays, characters are often dressed in seasonal outfits (Halloween, Christmas, and other special days).
• The Princess Fantasy Faire is the best way to take a photo with a Disney Princess.
• If you love villains, come during Halloween (mid-September through October 31st) to see more of them roaming the parks.
• Star Wars characters tend to stick to Tomorrowland in Disneyland. Chewbacca loves to give hugs but Darth Vader and Kylo Ren are quite intimidating!
• Marvel characters (like Spider-man and Captain America) often change. For instance, Thor makes appearances and Disney may introduce other Marvel characters to replace previous ones.

CHAPTER FOURTEEN

TIPS FOR VISITING WITH KIDS

Introduction

The Disneyland Resort is known for being the "The Happiest Place on Earth" and we truly believe that it is! Part of Walt Disney's vision was to provide a place for families to enjoy themselves with fun for everyone. Many of the rides at Disneyland are designed for the kid in us all, but this section is all about children from babies to ten-year-olds. Using this guide can help you have a pleasant stay with your children.

Note: *This section has brief ride descriptions aimed for the age group. For more descriptions, as well as Magic Tips on attractions and restaurant recommendations, see the full details on the resort pages.*

Babies and Toddlers

We hear a lot of parents asking if they should bring their baby to Disneyland. The answer is YES! Many parents love bringing their babies to the parks! If you decide to bring your baby to the resort, here is a list of what to bring, do, and all about the baby care centers.

What to Bring

Protection from the Sun - We recommend sunscreen, hats, blankets, and a covered stroller to keep your little one safe

Blankets and Warm Clothes - These items are essential for cooler days (or at night when the temperatures drop)

Diapers, Wipes, and a Change of Clothes - Just in case of a mess, a change of clothes can be a lifesaver

Bottles and Formula - Don't forget the liners!

Baby Food - The Disneyland Resort will allow small glass jars as long as they contain baby food

Backpack - This is for you to carry your baby's items. Sometimes you can hide these in a stroller, but just in case you leave your stroller for a ride, we recommend carrying your items with you

Stroller - Rentals start at $15 a day or bring your own. Fantasyland has several locations for parking your stroller while you wait in line. Cast Members patrol the area for safety.

The Disneyland Baby Care Center

Just in case you forget something, Disneyland is equipped with nannies that are there to help. Get baby food, diapers, wipes, and even medicine in these spots. They offer nursing rooms, changing tables, highchairs for feeding, a microwave, water, and more.

Baby Care Center Locations

Disneyland - Main Street, U.S.A., next to First Aid.

Disney California Adventure - In the Pacific Wharf, next to the Ghirardelli Store.

Changing Rooms - These are found in most restrooms (men and women).

Breast Feeding - Feeding your baby is a top priority and you shouldn't be nervous to do so at Disneyland. If you want privacy (or quiet), head to the Baby Care Centers in the parks.

First Aid - Located next to the Baby Care Center in Disneyland on Main Street, U.S.A.

Emergencies - If you experience an emergency, call 911.

Rides for Babies and Toddlers

"it's a small world" (Fantasyland) - A gentle boat ride with colors and singing children.

The Many Adventures of Winnie the Pooh (Critter Country) - A slow ride through the story of Winnie the Pooh. See his friends from Tigger to Piglet in this cute and florescent ride.

Dumbo the Flying Elephant (Fantasyland) - Circle round while flying on Dumbo. This ride was designed for kids, but the line can be long.

Mickey's Toontown - Meet Mickey, Minnie, Donald, and Goofy in this toddler-friendly zone. Also a great place for kid-friendly meals.

"a bug's land" (California Adventure) - Several gentle rides and a splash area perfectly designed for young kids. We recommend Heimlich's Chew Chew Train.

Carousels: King Triton's Carousel (California Adventure) and King Arthur's Carrousel (Disneyland) are two classic carousels, one in each park.

Jungle Cruise (Adventureland) - A slow moving boat through the African and Amazonian wilds

Pirates of the Caribbean - A long, dark ride on a boat with two drops at the beginning. If you think these will startle your baby, it's best to avoid it.

Disneyland Railroad - An easy ride around the perimeter of Disneyland

More Tips for Babies and Toddlers

See a Show or Parade - With wonderful music and dancing characters, your baby or toddler will be delighted. Disney Junior: Live on Stage (California Adventure) is a live stage show designed for toddlers. Check the map for a schedule of shows and parades.

Don't Try to Do It All - Young kids can love Disneyland, but that doesn't mean they'll have the energy for a continuous, all-day outing. Space out rides and times waiting in line for simple joys like looking at the baby ducks in the moat around Sleeping Beauty's Castle or eat a snack under some shade.

Take a Break - As a parent you know that babies and toddlers can wear out fast. At the Disneyland Resort, this is no exception. Plan to go back to the hotel, hang under the shade of trees or umbrellas, or find the Baby Care Center for some peace and quiet. When your baby is ready to go again, head back to the park until he or she is spent.

Rider Switch

Do you have a young child with you, but all of the adults in your party want to ride? Many Disneyland Resort rides give you the option to wait and switch places when finished.

Disneyland Locations

- Autopia
- Big Thunder Mountain Railroad
- Gadget's Go Coaster
- Indiana Jones Adventure
- Matterhorn Bobsleds
- Space Mountain
- Splash Mountain
- Star Tour - The Adventures Continue

California Adventure Locations

- California Screamin'
- Goofy's Sky School
- Grizzly River Run
- Luigi's Rollickin' Roadsters
- Jumpin' Jellyfish
- Mater's Junkyard Jamboree
- Radiator Springs Racers
- Silly Symphony Swings
- Soarin'
- Tuck and Roll's Drive 'Em Buggies

Kids (Ages 3-9)

Since every kid is different, their interests with Disneyland may vary greatly. Many children love fast rides while others look forward to meeting their favorite characters. With so much to do at the Disneyland Resort, we've narrowed it down to the best ideas.

In this section you will note the numbers next to the rides and attractions. We've numbered the rides in order of how kid-friendly they are. #1 will be the most kid friendly, and the higher numbers are less kid-friendly. The descriptions are there to help you make the best judgment for your child.

Disneyland with Kids

Main Street, U.S.A.

This land is filled with souvenir shops and places to eat.

Attractions

1. The Magic Shop - for fun games!
2. Horse-drawn street cars - for leisurely strolls
3. Visit the Gibson Girl Ice Cream Parlor for sweets.
4. Carnation Café is great for burgers, fries, and salads.

Dining

1. Plaza Inn - has character breakfasts with "Minnie and Friends" (book this early on Disneyland.com).

Fantasyland

This land has rides for all ages, but especially geared for kids.

Attractions

1. Fantasy Faire - Meet your favorite Disney Princesses.

2. Peter Pan's Flight, Pinocchio's Daring Journey, Snow White's Scary Adventures, Alice in Wonderland, and Mr. Toad's Wild Ride are all family-friendly "dark rides".
3. Storybook Land Canal Boats - A slow-moving guided boat ride around miniature sets from Disney movies.
4. Casey Jr. Circus Train - A slow-moving train ride through a green hillside and back.
5. Dumbo the Flying Elephant - Fly around and around while holding Dumbo's flying feather on this classic attraction.
6. Pixie Hollow - Meet Tinker Bell and her pixie friends.
7. Mad Tea Party - The classic Disneyland tea cups. You can control how fast you spin the tea cup by turning the wheel in the center.
8. The Matterhorn Bobsleds - If your child enjoys slower rollercoasters, the right side of the Matterhorn is less intense than the left. However, this ride does feature a scary Abominable Snowman (must be 42" / 107cm or taller).

Dining

1. Red Rose Taverne - Beauty and the Beast-themed burgers, pizzas, sandwiches, and French fries with plenty of seating to feed the family. We also recommend for dessert, the Grey Stuff – it's delicious!
2. Check out the popcorn and churro carts for some delicious treats for the kids.

Critter Country

A small, mostly kid-friendly land!

Attractions

1. The Many Adventures of Winnie the Pooh - Perfect for kids who love slow, colorful rides with happy critters.

2. Splash Mountain - You will get wet on this log ride with many drops and a massive one at the end! The theme is generally colorful and happy throughout (must be 40"/102cm or taller)

Dining

1. Hungry Bear Restaurant - A great place for families to eat. Plenty of picnic tables and a great selection of burgers, wraps, and entrees designed for kids.

Adventureland

A jungle-themed area with a couple of great attractions with kids and families in mind

Attractions

1. Tarzan's Treehouse™ - loved by kids who enjoy climbing.
2. Jungle Cruse - A riverboat ride designed for all ages.
3. Indiana Jones™ Adventure is perfect for kids who love thrill rides (must be 46"/117cm or taller).

Dining

3. Bengal Barbecue - Offers tasty snacks from breadsticks, pretzels, and skewers kids will love.

Mickey's Toontown

Another great area with characters, rides, and food designed for kids.

Attractions

1. Take a picture with Mickey and Minnie Mouse in their interactive homes.
2. Visit play areas for kids including Donald's Boat, Goofy's Playground, and Chip N' Dale Treehouse.
3. Toontown is filled with kid-friendly eateries and tables for eating.
4. Roger Rabbit's Car Toon Spin - a family-friendly "dark ride" with a wheel to spin the car.

5. Gadget's Go Coaster - a short, family-friendly rollercoaster with a typically long line (must be 35"/89cm to ride).

★ **Magic Tip** ★

Toontown is home to hot dogs, pizza, and kids' meals that are specially designed for each hungry child. See page 135.

New Orleans Square

This land is filled with great places to eat for those who enjoy creole and French dining.

Attractions

1. Pirates of the Caribbean - a music-filled pirate-themed boat ride with two drops at the beginning. Has many dark spots, but is generally not scary.
2. Haunted Mansion - a slow-moving ride through a haunted mansion that may frighten young kids

Dining

1. Café Orleans - Several choices for kids from macaroni and cheese to chicken breasts.

Frontierland

Jump into the wild west in this land filled with runaway trains, cowboys, and plenty of space for families to eat!

Attractions

1. Pirate's Lair on Tom Sawyer's Island - An island playground with bridges and hiding spots designed for kids of all ages. You must take a raft to the island and back.
2. Big Thunder Mountain - A fast-moving rollercoaster labeled "the wildest ride in the wilderness". This is a family-friendly rollercoaster with no loops or big drops (must be 40"/102cm or taller).

Dining

1. The Golden Horseshoe is a perfect restaurant with plenty of seating for the whole family as well as options for kids' meals (Chicken Nuggets or the Power Pack).

Tomorrowland

While this land is known for its thrills, Tomorrowland offers a variety of rides and attractions for the entire family.

Attractions

1. Finding Nemo Submarine Voyage - A family-friendly slow-moving ride in a submarine starring Nemo and his friends. Not recommended for those who don't enjoy enclosed spaces.
2. Jedi Training Academy - A live show where kids (ages 4 - 12) can volunteer to become Jedis and battle Darth Vader. Look on the map for show times and you can eat at the Galactic Grill while watching the show.
3. Star Wars Launch Bay - meet and take a photo with Chewbacca or Kylo Ren, see prop replicas from *The Force Awakens*, and shop *Star Wars* collectables.
4. Astro Orbiter - A spinning rocket ride similar to Dumbo the Flying Elephant.
5. Buzz Lightyear Astro Blasters - A slow-moving family-friendly "dark ride" where riders shoot a laser gun at targets to rack up points.
6. Autopia - A ride where kids can drive cars around a track (must be 32"/81cm to drive and 54"/137cm or taller to drive alone).
7. *Star Tours*: The Adventures Continue - A 3D motion simulation ride through two scenes inspired by *Star Wars*. Contains loud noises and lighting effects (must be 40"/102cm or taller to ride).
8. Space Mountain - A fast-moving rollercoaster in the dark. (must be 40"/102cm or taller to ride)

Dining

9. Redd Rockett's Pizza Port - Cafeteria Style pizza, salads, pasta, sweets, and drinks with plenty of indoor and outdoor seating.
10. Galactic Grill - Hamburgers, fries, and meals for kids served hot at this fast service restaurant with plenty of tables and seats.

California Adventure with Kids

Buena Vista Street

This land is filled with souvenir shops and places to eat.

Attractions

1. Red Car Trolley - A slow ride to Hollywood Land that young children may enjoy.

2. The Pixar Play Parade - Watch your favorite Pixar characters in this upbeat dance and music parade. Check the map for show times.

Dining

1. Visit Clarabelle's Hand-Scooped Ice Cream for sweets.

"a bug's land"

A kid-friendly land stylized from Pixar's *A Bug's Life*.

Attractions

1. *It's Tough to be a Bug*! - A hilarious 3D theatre show designed for the whole family.
2. Flik's Fun Fair - A collection of rides designed for kids of all ages. However, young thrill riders may not enjoy this land.
    - Heimlich's Chew Chew Train - A funny ride on a caterpillar through his favorite scented foods.
    - Francis' Ladybug Boogie - Spinning ladybug cars.
    - Princess Dot Puddle Park - Perfect for kids who love to get wet! Luckily, it's located next to a bathroom for easy drying.
    - Flik's Flyers - Move around in a circles in the sky on simulated hot air balloons.
    - Tuck and Roll's Drive 'Em Buggies - Kid-sized bumper cars.

Paradise Pier

The largest land of Disney California Adventure, based around a waterfront and home of definitive rides and the spectacular World of Color night show.

Attractions

1. World of Color - A stunning nighttime water show filled with Disney characters and color that's a perfect fit for the entire family.

2. The Little Mermaid: Ariel's Undersea Adventure - A family-friendly slow-moving "dark ride" through the story and music of Disney's *The Little Mermaid*.
3. King Triton's Carousel - A classic carousel with fish instead of horses.
4. Golden Zephyr - A slow-moving ship that spins in circles on a cable. This is family-friendly and perfect for toddlers, however, could be boring for kids who enjoy thrill rides.

5. Mickey's Fun Wheel - A Ferris wheel with two different experiences. For kids who love thrill rides, choose a swinging gondola. For kids that don't like fast movement, choose a stationary gondola. Not recommended for children who do not enjoy heights.
6. Toy Story Midway Mania! - A 4D target practice based on Pixar's *Toy Story*. Kids of all ages will enjoy this ride, though not recommended for those that have trouble seeing with 3D glasses.

7. Jumpin' Jellyfish - Older children will enjoy these dropping jellyfish. Not recommended for those who don't enjoy heights (must be 40"/102cm or taller).
8. Silly Symphony Swings - Spin around over land and water on these orchestrated swings. Not recommended for children who do not enjoy heights, but perfect for preteens and adventurous kids (must be 40"/102cm).
9. Goofy's Sky School - A kid-friendly rollercoaster with sharp turns and small dips. Younger kids might not like this ride for its slight thrill factor. Also keep in mind that larger adults sometimes have a difficult time fitting into these seats (must be 42"/107cm or taller).
10. California Screamin' - A high-speed rollercoaster for the adventurous kids with larger dips and a loop (must be 48"/122cm to ride)

Dining

1. Boardwalk Pizza and Pasta - Serves up hot pizzas, salads, and kid-sized meatball sandwiches.

Cars Land

Set to the beautiful, mountainous landscape of Route 66, Cars Land is as breathtaking as it is fun for the entire family.

Attractions

1. Mater's Junkyard Jamboree - Flick and turn on this unpredictable ride. Perfect for kids who enjoy fast-moving rides (must be 32"/81cm or taller to ride).
2. Luigi's Rollickin' Roadsters - A new attraction where cars dance and turn to the music. Perfect for kids (must be 32"/81cm or taller to ride).
3. Radiator Springs Racers - Race along the stars of Pixar's *Cars* in this "dark ride" and thrill ride combination that the entire family will love. It is not recommended for those who don't enjoy fast-moving rides (must be 40"/102cm or taller)

Dining

1. Cozy Cone Motel - Pick up snacks in orange traffic cones from churros, drinks, soft-serve ice cream, queso, pretzel bites, frozen drinks, and popcorn.
2. Fillmore's Taste-In - A fruit and beverage cart.
3. Flo's V8 Café - A diner with plenty of indoor and outdoor seating. Breakfast - Scrambled Eggs, Turkey Bacon, Potatoes, and fruit or a fruit plate with yogurt and a bran muffin. Lunch/Dinner - Roast Beef Sandwich, Turkey Sandwich, or Macaroni and Cheese.

Pacific Wharf

A land reminiscent of San Francisco wharfs. This area is filled with food mainly aimed at adults, however most have great options for kids.

1. Cocina Cucamonga Mexican Grill - Serves chicken and ride toddler meal plus kids' meals with a bean cheese burrito or chicken quesadilla
2. Lucky Fortune Cookery - Asian food with a kids' meal featuring chicken and brown rice
3. Pacific Wharf Distribution Co. - toddler meal of cheesy macaroni, kids' meal with turkey sandwich or "power pack" with smoothie, apples, carrots, banana, and crackers.

Hollywood Land

From glamour, film studios, and decrepit buildings, this land captures the true spirit of Hollywood.

Attractions

1. Monsters, Inc. Mike and Sulley to the Rescue! - A "dark ride" with vibrant colors following the story of Pixar's *Monsters, Inc.* Kids of all ages will enjoy this ride, though young thrill riders may want to skip it.
2. Disney Animation Building Attractions

a. *Turtle Talk with Crush* - A hilarious interactive show designed for kids 3-9.
b. Sorcerer's Workshop - Make your own animation and record your voice over a Disney film.
c. Animation Academy - Learn to draw a Disney character from a live Disney Cartoonist. Older kids may find more enjoyment from this classroom environment.

<u>Dining</u>

1. Award Wieners - Hot dogs and more. Also available are kids' power packs for a healthier option
2. Schmoozies - Delicious fruit smoothies.
3. Fairfax Market - A fruit and beverage snack stand

Grizzly Peak

Venture into California's wilderness, complete with redwoods and roaring rapids, all surrounding a bear-shaped mountain.

<u>Attractions</u>

1. Redwood Challenge Trail - Kids can climb, play, and earn badges by completing tasks.
2. Soarin' - A hang glider simulation for the entire family. Not recommended for those who don't enjoy heights or brief periods of darkness (must be 40"/102cm or taller).
3. Grizzly River Run - A raft-based rapids adventure ending in a giant splash. Not recommended for those who don't enjoy getting wet or big drops (must be 40"/102cm or taller to ride)

<u>Dining</u>

1. Smokejumpers Grill - American hamburgers and more. Featured <u>kids' meals</u> with chicken nuggets, kid's hamburger, or a "power pack" with a smoothie, apples, carrots, banana, and crackers.

CHAPTER FIFTEEN

ADULT GUIDE

Introduction

The Disneyland Resort may be family-friendly but that doesn't mean it can't also an adult retreat. From luxury hotels and fine-dining to thrill rides and a dive bar, the Disneyland Resort has plenty to entertain adults! In this section we outline grown-up activities from the best places to drink to avoiding families with children.

Note: *The Disneyland Park does not serve alcohol, however, Disney California Adventure and Downtown Disney have many options for wine, beer, and cocktails (must be 21 years of age or older with a valid ID to consume alcoholic beverages)*

Parents' Evening Out

If you're an adult with children, part of your perfect Disneyland Resort vacation might be a night without them. If you're interested in heading back to the parks, Disneyland and California Adventure are often open until midnight. Or, perhaps you'd settle for a dinner alone with your significant other.

Bars and Drinks

Would it surprise you to hear that there is a Disney-themed dive bar at the Disneyland Hotel and that it's *awesome*? Check out our recommendations of the best places to drink while at the Disneyland Resort:

<u>**Trader Sam's Enchanted Tiki Bar**</u> - *Top Choice!*
Location: Disneyland Hotel (pool area)
Description: Island-themed dive bar
Price: $$
Why We Recommend It: Dim lighting, air conditioning, and scraggly bartenders serve excellent drinks and bar food in this unique setting. Try a specialty cocktail or order a beer on draft. Certain drinks cause the room's volcanoes to erupt or brew a storm!

★ **Magic Tips** ★

1. Bring the kids in the daytime if you'd like!
2. After 8pm, Trader Sam's is 21 and older only
3. Trader Sam's also has a secret menu including a delicious alcoholic Dole whip!

Cove Bar - *Top Choice!*
Location: Disney California Adventure, Paradise Pier
Description: Casual Lounge with a full bar and extensive wine selection
Price: $$
Why We Recommend It: A great place to take it easy and enjoy a specialty cocktail or glass of wine while inside of the park. The Cove Bar is outdoors but covered, and has excellent views of the boardwalk with the California Scream' Rollercoaster.

★ **Magic Tip** ★

1. Get there early to avoid lines. The Cove Bar is a popular destination, but before 11.30am, you can have a great snack of Lobster Nachos or other bar food and start drinking without the lines.
2. The Cove Bar has a secret menu! Check out these items
   a. Fun Wheel - a colorful layer of vodka, gin, light rum, passion fruit liqueur, and blue curacao. Perfect if you like sweet and sour drinks
   b. Black Pearl - Vodka and rum with sprite and sweet and sour, for those craving a drink of their inner pirate
   c. Neverland Tea - Vodka, gin, rum, peach schnapps, and many other colorful mixes to help you fly with the pixies!
   d. There are even more! Ask for the secret menu!

ESPN Zone (Bar)
Location: Downtown Disney
Description: Sports Bar with a full menu
Price: $$
Why We Recommend It: Choose from a full bar with beer on draft while you watch sports on one of 120 HD screens.

Napa Rose Lounge

Location: Disney's Grand California Hotel and Spa

Description: Casual Lounge with a full bar and extensive wine selection

Price: $$

Why We Recommend It: A wine-lover's Disneyland dream! The Napa Rose Lounge is perfect for taking a break from the rides as you sit back and relax while you sip wine or nibble on excellent appetizers.

The Lounge at Steakhouse 55

Location: Disneyland Hotel

Description: Casual Lounge with a full bar and extensive wine selection

Price: $$

Why We Recommend It: The casual lounge and bar of the Disneyland Hotel. It's much cleaner and nicer than Trader Sam's, but serves its Disney charm with mouthwatering appetizers and a full bar with wine selections.

Carthay Circle Lounge

Location: Disney California Adventure, Buena Vista Street

Description: Casual Lounge with a full bar and extensive wine selection.

Price: $$

Why We Recommend It: A great place to take it easy and enjoy a specialty cocktail or glass of wine while inside the park.

Rita's Baja Blenders

Location: Disney California Adventure, Pacific Wharf

Description: A stand with delicious margaritas and sangria.

Price: $

Why We Recommend It: Order a drink that you can carry with you around the park (you must finish it before you get on a ride, but you can wait in line with it).

⋆ **Magic Tip** ⋆ For a double shot of tequila, ask for the Grand Margarita.

Pacific Wharf Distribution Co.

Location: Disney California Adventure, Pacific Wharf

Description: A stand with an assortment of craft beers.

Price: $

Why We Recommend It: Order a beer that you can carry with you around the park (you must finish it before you get on a ride, but you can wait in line with it).

⋆ **Magic Tip** ⋆ The line can look long, but the servers pour fast so you won't be waiting long.

Wine Country Trattoria

Location: Disney California Adventure, Pacific Wharf

Description: Wine and wine flights on a terrace.

Price: $$

Why We Recommend It: Excellent wine and magnificent views of Pacific Wharf.

⋆ **Magic Tip** ⋆ Book a World of Color package and drink wine before watching the show from reserved seating (book at Disneyland.com or call 714-781-3463).

Restaurants with Alcohol

Disney California Adventure

Alfresco Tasting Terrace - Disney Family of Wines.
Ariel's Grotto - full bar, specialty cocktails, and draft beers.
Bayside Brews - craft beer on draft and wine.
Carthay Circle Lounge - full bar with specialty cocktails
Carthay Circle Restaurant - Disney Family of Wines and cocktails.
Cove Bar - full bar, specialty cocktails, beer, and wine.
Mendocino Terrace - large selections of wines and beer.
Sonoma Terrace - wine and craft beer selection.
Wine Country Trattoria - wine and wine flights, cocktails, sangria, and domestic beer.

Downtown Disney

Catal Restaurant - Wine, specialty cocktails, draft and beers
ESPN Zone - Full bar and beer on draft
La Brea Bakery Café - Wines, bottled and draft beers.
Naples Ristorante e Pizzeria - Specialty cocktails, wines, and domestic beer.
Rainforest Cafe - Wines and domestic beer.
Ralph Brennan's Jazz Kitchen - Specialty cocktails.
Tortilla Jo's - Specialty Margaritas, beer, specialty cocktails, and wines.
Uva Bar - A full bar with an extensive beer and wine list and specialty cocktails.

Disneyland Park

The are no options here for standard guests. Disney kept it this way to keep Walt's vision alive for a family-friendly park.

How to Avoid Children

Okay, it's impossible to see absolutely no children at the Disneyland Resort, but you can avoid being around the bulk of them. We've listed some great tips on how to stay clear of families with small children at the parks.

Note: *We've noticed that children 10 and older are generally very well-behaved at Disneyland. You may not even notice them as they are excited and stimulated by the sights just like you will be. Nevertheless, as promised, the tips:*

1. Visit Trader Sam's Enchanted Tiki Bar after 8PM - no one under 21 is allowed in Trader Sam's after 8PM. You can drink from a full bar, eat, and lounge in this dive bar located in the Disneyland Hotel pool area (non-guests are allowed).

2. Stay Away from Fantasyland and Mickey's Toon Town - these kid-friendly lands are typically filled with small children. If you'd like to avoid them, we recommend staying away at all costs. However, the Matterhorn Bobsleds are great (the height restriction keeps the tiny children at bay).

3. Say "no" to Parades - these attractions are like magnets for small children. You've been warned.

4. Ride During a Parade - if you must ride a Fantasyland attraction, these are the best times! The families will flock to the parade route, generally leaving adults behind to wait for these popular rides. Check your park map for parade times.

5. Eat at a Bar - The Cove Bar in California and Carthay Circle Lounge are two of many places in Disney California Adventure that are generally kid-free (or have far fewer children than other places).

6. Eat at the Blue Bayou (Disneyland) - This table service restaurant is generally quiet and kid-free. Don't forget to make a reservation before you go!

7. Don't enter "a bug's land" (Disney California Adventure) - this is the kid-friendly zone that will make any child-avoiding adult cringe.

8. Stay away from Redd Rocket's Pizza Port in Tomorrowland. This place is typically filled with kids eager to run around tables while they devour pizza.

9. Pay attention to height requirements because children are generally small, these restrictions can instantly weed them out at the start of the queue.

10. Attractions to Avoid
    In Disneyland
    - Astro Orbiter
    - Autopia
    - Buzz Lightyear Astro Blaster
    - Fantasyland

- Finding Nemo Submarine Voyage
- Mickey's Toon Town
- The Many Adventures of Winnie the Pooh
- Tarzan's Treehouse
- Pirate's Lair on Tom Sawyer Island

In California Adventure

- "a bug's land"
- Golden Zephyr
- Goofy's Sky School
- Jumpin' Jellyfish
- King Triton's Carousel
- The Little Mermaid
- Monsters, Inc. Mike & Sulley to the Rescue!
- Red Car Trolley
- Redwood Creek Challenge Trial
- Silly Symphony Swings
- *Turtle Talk with Crush*

Downtown Disney for Adults

There are many things to do in Downtown Disney that adults will love, from movies to shopping and even seeing a rock concert or a live DJ!

1. **Watch a Movie** - AMC Theatres offers a wide selection of movies. Visit **www.amctheatres.com** for show times.
2. **Go Shopping** - Buy surf gear at Quicksilver or makeup at Sephora.

3. **Lounge at Starbucks** - With free Wi-Fi and drink favorites you can spend time on their massive patio as people stroll by.
4. **See a Free Concert** - Musicians love Downtown Disney. They rent the stages and booths to perform nightly concerts.
5. **Go Bowling** - Splitsville comes to Downtown Disney late-2017/early 2018! The place is swanky, fun, and even has great food!

Smoking Sections

There are a total of 5 smoking areas at the Disneyland Parks and 6 near the Disneyland Hotels. Also, the Disneyland Resort considers e-cigarettes to be "smoking". Downtown Disney allows smoking but with restrictions (see next page).

Disneyland Smoking

1. Main Entry Plaza - The esplanade between Disneyland and Disney California Adventure.
2. Tomorrowland - Look for this section near Autopia and the train station.
3. Frontierland - Almost directly across from The Haunted Mansion.

Note: *During Mickey's Halloween Party (a separate event held September through October, the will not be any smoking inside of the park. Instead, you will have to leave to the esplanade (the space between the two parks) to smoke and re-enter when you have finished.*

Disney California Adventure Smoking

1. Hollywood Land - Look for the area near the Monsters, Inc. ride.
2. Grizzly Peak - Follow the trail behind the Grizzly River Run.

Disneyland Hotel Smoking

1. Adventure Tower - On the southeast corner.
2. Fantasy Tower - On the northwest corner.
3. Frontier Tower - On the south side.

Disney's Grand Californian Hotel and Spa

1. Outdoor - Near the Hearthstone Lounge.
2. Courtyard - On the opposite side of Sephora, inside of the hotel courtyard.

Disney's Paradise Pier Hotel

The closest smoking section is the Frontier Tower at the Disneyland Hotel (located on the south side).

Downtown Disney

You make smoke in Downtown Disney, but not in the restrooms, stores, or near the restaurants.

CHAPTER SIXTEEN

A NON-RIDER'S GUIDE

Introduction

Typically, the first thing that people think about at Disneyland is the castle. The second thought is usually the rides. But what if you or your guest don't enjoy the drops, turns, and twists. Are there things for you to do? Would you enjoy yourself? Would it be worth the money? In short, is the Disneyland Resort for you? The answer is YES! The attractions at the resort aren't all rides. In fact, most of them are shows, sights to see, activities, and more that are accessible by everyone! Disneyland and California Adventure are sure to offer something for everyone.

Recommendations

1. **See the sights** - Disneyland and Disney California Adventure are something to behold. They offer intricate architecture, well-planned lands, and lush, meticulously manicured foliage.
2. **Sample gourmet food** - Dazzle your senses with savory meals and sweet treats all around the parks, hotels, and Downtown Disney.
3. **See a show** - The Disneyland Resort is known for magnificent shows and parades
4. **Meet Characters** - Take a photo with your favorite Disney character. Or watch the many musical bands playing around the park.
5. **Ride a slow-moving attraction** - Some rides don't have drops or move fast, many of them can be perfect for your speed as you experience the magnificent stories these rides have to offer.
6. **Shop!** - There are stores on every corner of the parks.
7. **Get a Princess Makeover at the Bibbidi Bobbidi Boutique** - perfect for kids who want to dress as their favorite Disney Princess. There are also options to become a pirate or a knight!
8. **People Watch** - this will either sound fun or creepy to you, but Disneyland has some unique visitors in creative outfits, or watch them plummet from Splash Mountain!

Recommended Shows and Parades

1. World of Color (Disney California Adventure)
2. "Fantasy In The Sky" Fireworks (Disneyland)

3. Paint the Night Parade (California Adventure)
4. Jedi Training (Disneyland)
5. Fantasy Faire (Disneyland)
6. Mickey and the Magical Map (Disneyland)
7. Laughing Stock Co. (Disneyland)
8. See the Disney classic, *Steamboat Willie* at the Main Street Cinema (Disneyland).

Best of the Slow Rides and Attractions

These attractions don't have drops or move quickly at all. Here are some you may enjoy (in order):

1. Explore the Disney Animation Building (Disney California Adventure) - learn to draw and see how the animators bring Disney classics to life!
2. Heimlich's Chew Chew Train (Disney California Adventure) - a slow-moving train with humor and delicious aromas.
3. Peter Pan's Flight (Disneyland) - see the story of *Peter Pan* while flying in a slow-moving pirate ship.
4. Jungle Cruise (Disneyland) - a humorous tour guide takes you on a riverboat through the Amazon and Africa.
5. Alice in Wonderland (Disneyland) - a classic "dark ride" through the story of Disney's *Alice in Wonderland*.
6. The Little Mermaid ~ Ariel's Undersea Adventure (California Adventure) - a slow-moving "dark ride" that explores the story of Disney's *The Little Mermaid*.
7. Haunted Mansion (Disneyland) - a slow-moving "dark ride" through a haunted house.
8. "it's a small world" (Disneyland) - the classic, slow-paced boat ride around the world.

Other Fun without Rides

1. Order a pair of customized Mickey Ears with your name on them (Disneyland)
2. Try to lift the sword in the stone (Disneyland - Fantasyland, near the carousel)
3. Check out the Disney Gallery on Main Street, U.S.A. (Disneyland)
4. Look for Push the Talking Trashcan (Disneyland - Tomorrowland)
5. Play the Fun Wheel Challenge right before World of Color (California Adventure)
6. Watch the Dapper Dans, a barbershop quartet, perform on Main Street, U.S.A. (Disneyland)
7. Look at the vegetables that grow in Tomorrowland (Disneyland)
8. Book a backstage tour and see how the magic is created. Call (714) 781-8687.

CHAPTER SEVENTEEN

FASTPASS, MAXPASS AND SINGLE RIDER TIPS

In 1999, Disneyland first implemented a type of virtual queuing system that skips the hassle of waiting in long lines. FastPass distribution kiosks allow you to reserve and cut a large section of the line without an additional cost! The most popular rides in Disneyland and California Adventure have FastPass kiosks, and you're given a reservation ticket to remind you of a return time.

FastPass is your best bet to skipping the lines and experiencing the most attractions during your stay. However, there is a strategy that makes FastPass even more efficient to use. In this chapter, we review special hacks that will maximize your park experience using Disneyland's FastPass system!

MaxPass Pros and Cons

Disneyland first implemented its MaxPass system mid-2017 in order to give guests the opportunity to use their mobile devices to reserve FastPass selection for an additional cost, starting at $10. This new feature, however, was met with wide criticism as guests at Walt Disney World can use the app to book FastPass for free. However, MaxPass also gives its users the ability to download unlimited amounts of their professional park photos as well as book FastPass for both California Adventure and Disneyland. While this new feature is handy, it may not be for everyone, including the thrifty traveler. Here we've detailed the pros and cons of MaxPass, along with our recommendations.

Pros of MaxPass

1. **Less Walking** - No need to run to Space Mountain or Guardians of the Galaxy - Mission Breakout! Instead, use your mobile device and select the next available FastPass slot.
2. **Early Booking** - MaxPass often allows earlier timeslots and sometimes even exclusive availability for FastPass. For example, if the next FastPass time slot is available at 4PM - 5PM, those with MaxPass might be able to get a FastPass earlier at 3PM - 4PM.
3. **Use for Both Parks** - The single cost of MaxPass works for both parks, so if you are park hopping, you don't have to physically move to the other park to retrieve a FastPass. This can save you a lot of time and save your legs for the rest of the day!
4. **PhotoPass Is Included** - Other than getting your FastPasses on the application, MaxPass is great for the best photos. Download any professional Disney photos you get from around the park, including snaps taken by cameras on the rides! Then you can freely post them on your social media or share them with friends. There's really nothing else like it!
5. **Cancel FastPass** - If you have MaxPass, you are able to change your FastPass reservations, including cancelling one from your mobile device.

Cons of MaxPass

1. **It Costs Extra** - Starting at $10 per person, you'll need to actually purchase this feature separate for each person in your group to use its full potential. If you are

just using it for the PhotoPass feature, just have one person purchase MaxPass in your group
2. **FastPass is Still Free** - You don't need MaxPass to get a FastPass. The kiosks for physical FastPass tickets are right next to the rides that offer it. We cover these spots in this section.

Recommendation

We would use MaxPass for 2 reasons

1. If you want to use the Disney PhotoPass, this is the cheapest option
2. If you have eager riders who want to experience the most out of Disneyland, MaxPass will optimize their experience without running all over the resort.

How to use MaxPass

We would use MaxPass for 2 reasons
1. Download the Disneyland app on your mobile device
2. You'll need to physically be inside of the park to get prompted to use MaxPass
3. Tap the blue Mickey head at the bottom of the app, select "Get FastPass" and then "Get Started" to purchase the MaxPass
4. Each person in your group will need MaxPass if you are using it for more than just the PhotoPass feature.

FastPast Hacks

FastPass is the best way to maximize your stay at the Disneyland Resort. This free feature uses a ticketing system to use with select rides and attractions at both parks. We are here to share the best hacks with you!

FastPass Stacking at Disneyland

Note: *We only recommend this hack for those familiar with the Disneyland FastPass system*

To many Disneyland enthusiasts, grabbing as many FastPasses at once is an art form. We call it "FastPass Stacking" because it allows you to get a ton of FastPasses at the same time and ride multiple rides in a short period of time. This is a bit tricky, but if you have the energy, it's entirely possible to experience the best rides at Disneyland quickly. The hack works because Disneyland allows you to get a FastPass for a ride as long as it's after the start of your ride time. Since the start time of the FastPasses is immediate once the park opens, you can grab as many as you can until the time switches.

Keep in mind that there are restrictions. Sometimes you'll have to wait 10-20 minutes before grabbing the next FastPass selection. Also, you cannot grab a FastPass for the same ride twice in a row until the timeslot is over.

To maximize your FastPass stacking, you must get to the park before the "rope" drops at Disneyland. Then, cruise over to your choice of FastPass kiosk or use the MaxPass on the Disneyland application. How many can you stack?!

Get Disconnected

A "disconnected FastPass" is one that doesn't interfere with you collecting FastPass. For example, if you get a FastPass to World of Color it will not affect you getting another FastPass for a different attraction. When you grab a FastPass to these night-time shows, you can immediately grab another FastPass to a second attraction. You can also get a FastPass to both of these shows if you'd like. However, a ride like Space Mountain will affect your ability to get another FastPass until your ride time or 2 hours has passed, whichever comes first.

Note: *Again, to save your feet some time, we'd recommend a MaxPass or sending out your most energetic party member with all of your tickets to grab FastPasses. Of course, if you're traveling between parks, your entire party needs to join them.*

Cancel Your FastPass

Sometimes plans change or you see that a line is shorter than expected. Remember that if you have MaxPass, you can cancel your FastPass on the Disneyland app!

FastPast Locations

Disneyland

Big Thunder Mountain Railroad - To the right of the regular line in Frontierland.
Necessity: Medium

Haunted Mansion - To the left of the ride line gates in New Orleans Square.
Necessity: Low

Indiana Jones Adventure - Between the ride line and Jungle Cruise in Adventureland.
Necessity: High

Matterhorn Bobsleds - Across from the main line queue, tucked in a corner. You'll see a cast member or two standing beside wooden boxes with carved animals on top. Those are the FastPass machines.
Necessity: Medium

Roger Rabbit's Car Toon Spin - At the FastPass sign near the ride in Mickey's Toontown.
Necessity: Low

Space Mountain - To the right of the regular queue in Tomorrowland. Sometimes there is a separate line for the FastPass, hold close to the right side.
Necessity: High

Splash Mountain - Across from The Many Adventures of Winnie the Pooh in Critter Country.
Necessity: High (Low on cold days)

Star Tours: The Adventures Continue - Across from the queue, next to Buzz Lightyear Astro Blasters in Tomorrowland.
Necessity: Medium

California Adventure

California Screamin' - To the left of the queue in Paradise Pier.
Necessity: Medium

Guardians of the Galaxy - Mission: Breakout - Across from ride queue in Hollywood Land.
Necessity: Very High

Goofy's Sky School - To the right of the queue in Paradise Pier.
Necessity: Low

Grizzly River Run - To the left of the queue in Grizzly Peak.
Necessity: Medium (High on hot days, Low on cold days)

Radiator Springs Racers - Near *It's Tough to be a Bug!* in "a bug's land". Sometimes the FastPass line will continue into Buena Vista Street, especially on busier days.
Necessity: High

Soarin' - To the left the queue in Grizzly Peak.
Necessity: Medium

Toy Story Midway Mania - Across from the ride, but between the Ferris wheel and California Scream' coaster
Necessity: High

World of Color - Look for the kiosks near The Little Mermaid ride in Paradise Pier. This will not affect you selecting other FastPass times.
Necessity: High

Single Rider Line Spots

The single ride line is designed for those willing to ride alone in a row of strangers. Disney is all about efficacy, and sometimes rides have an off-number seats per row (like the Radiator Spring Racers), so filling in that extra space loads more people at a time. The benefit to the rider is a quicker way onto the attraction as Disney uses a specialized line for single riders. Only a handful of rides in each park has this feature. While the line often saves time, many instances it doesn't (the Indiana Jones Adventure is often known for this). However, if you're lucky and in a single line with your party, you might get seated together! Either way, we highly recommend this for teens and adults, but not so much families with younger kids who wouldn't be seated with a guardian.

Disneyland

Indiana Jones Adventure - Ask the Cast Member at the queue start for a Single Rider pass. You'll be instructed to the single rider line from there.
Splash Mountain - This is a bit hidden and located by walking through the exit of the ride until you reach a Cast Member to ask about the Single Rider Line.
Matterhorn Bobsleds - It's the same line as the FastPass return, but the cast members will split you up before heading onto the ride.

California Adventure

California Screamin' - Another hidden line (though it's marked with a blue sign) located by walking through the left side of the queue where you will see a gate (it takes you to the opposite side of the rollercoaster boarding)

Soarin' Over California - At the FastPass entrance, ask a Cast Member for the Single Rider Line.

Grizzly River Run - Move up the exit stairs and meet the Cast Members at the rotating platform to ask about the Single Rider Line.

Radiator Springs Racers - A clearly marked queue at the start of the queues.

Goofy's Sky School - Look for the yellow sign near the start of the queue and by the FastPass line.

CHAPTER EIGHTEEN
FREE STUFF

Introduction

You can get some great souvenirs and treats for free at the Disneyland Resort. Of course, you still have to pay for your ticket, but these are great things that you can eat, take home with you, or use along the way.

List of Free Items

Special Occasion Pin – Celebrate your birthday, anniversary, and more with a free pin (Disneyland, and no they don't card you on your birthday).

Stickers – Take a survey near the entrance to the parks and ask for a sticker.

Chocolate - Get a free chocolate square when you enter (Disney California Adventure).

Boudin Bread - During the Boudin Factory Tour each guest receives a free piece of sample bread (Disney California Adventure).

Disney Art - Learn to draw your favorite Disney characters from and keep the paper at the Animation Academy in California Adventure.

Professional Photos - Stop at any of the photo booths scattered around the park and ask the Disneyland photographer to take a photo with your camera. They are happy to do so and typically they do a great job! (Disneyland and California Adventure)

Extra FastPasses - If you have an interest in the Disney Vacation Club (or even if you don't), they offer three free FastPasses to each person in your group for watching the 60-90-minute presentation. These can be used at either park for any ride except the Radiator Springs Racers. (Downtown Disney)

Maps - This might be a no-brainer, but maps are great souvenirs, especially since they have the surrounding dates of your arrival. These are located at the entrances to Disneyland and California Adventure.

CHAPTER NINETEEN
DISNEYLAND RESORT - TOP 10 LISTS

Introduction

The Disneyland Resort has seemingly endless attractions, sights, and food to enjoy. We can understand if you feel overwhelmed deciding what to do! Don't worry because we're coming to the rescue with our most recommended things to do during your stay at Disneyland.

Listed in Order

(#1 being the most recommended)

Best Thrill Rides

1. Guardians of the Galaxy - Mission: Breakout! (California Adventure)
2. Indiana Jones Adventure (Disneyland)
3. California Screamin' Rollercoaster (California Adventure)
4. Space Mountain (Disneyland)

5. Radiator Springs Racers (California Adventure)
6. Splash Mountain (Disneyland)
7. Big Thunder Mountain Railroad (Disneyland)
8. Star Tours - The Adventures Continue (Disneyland)
9. Goofy's Sky School (California Adventure)
10. Grizzly River Run (California Adventure)

Best Family Rides

1. Toy Story Midway Mania (California Adventure)
2. Pirates of the Caribbean (Disneyland)
3. Peter Pan's Flight (Disneyland)
4. Star Tours - The Adventures Continue (Disneyland)
5. Haunted Mansion (Disneyland)
6. Jungle Cruise (Disneyland)
7. "it's a small world" (Disneyland)
8. Heimlich's Chew Chew Train (California Adventure)
9. Dumbo the Flying Elephant (Disneyland)
10. Mater's Junkyard Jamboree (California Adventure)

Best Slow-Moving Rides for Kids

1. Peter Pan's Flight (Disneyland)
2. The Little Mermaid (California Adventure)
3. Toy Story Midway Mania! (California Adventure)
4. Dumbo the Flying Elephant (Disneyland)
5. Alice in Wonderland (Disneyland)
6. Mad Tea Party (Disneyland)
7. The Many Adventures of Winnie the Pooh (Disneyland)
8. Storybook Land Canal Boats (Disneyland)
9. Heimlich's Chew Chew Train (California Adventure)
10. Finding Nemo Submarine Voyage (Disneyland)

Best Non-Ride Attractions

1. Frozen - Live at the Hyperion (California Adventure)
2. World of Color (Disneyland)
3. Paint the Night Parade (California Adventure)

4. Fantasmic! (Disneyland)
5. *It's Tough to be a Bug!* (California Adventure)
6. Animation Academy (California Adventure)
7. Mickey and the Magical Map (Disneyland)
8. Sorcerer's Workshop (California Adventure)
9. Enchanted Tiki Room (Disneyland)
10. Sleeping Beauty Castle Walkthrough (Disneyland)

Best Food

1. Monte Cristo Sandwich (Disneyland - Blue Bayou Restaurant and Café Orleans)
2. Dole Whip (Disneyland - Tiki Juice Bar)
3. Lobster Nachos (California Adventure, Cove Bar)
4. Churros (Disneyland and California Adventure)
5. Corn Dog (Disneyland, Little Red Wagon Corn Dogs and California Adventure, Corn Dog Castle)
6. Mickey-Shaped Waffle (Disneyland, Carnation Café)
7. Clam Chowder in a Sourdough Bread Bowl (Disneyland, French Market Restaurant and California Adventure, Pacific Wharf Café)
8. Lobster Roll (Disneyland, Harbour Galley)
9. Chili Cheese Dog (Disneyland, Refreshment Corner)
10. Mickey-Shaped Beignets (Disneyland, Mint Julep Bar)

Note: *Look for the "Top Choice!" in the restaurant descriptions for our most recommended.*

CHAPTER TWENTY

HIDDEN MICKEYS

Introduction

It's no secret that Walt Disney loved his cartoon mouse, Mickey. Ever since he created the character in the 1920's, Mickey has found his way into nearly every piece of Walt Disney's creations from films to logos to them parks. Now, you might be thinking *Mickey Mouse isn't in Cinderella or Aladdin!* - where, in fact, he is- or, at least, his image is. You know that famous logo of the Mickey ears? It's just three circles, a large one for the face and two smaller ones for the ears. Well, these show up *everywhere* from the bubbles while Cinderella scrubbed the floors during her labors to a quick scene where Jasmine's pet tiger, Raja, changes briefly into a Mickey-like head. Even *Frozen* has a Mickey doll in a bookcase in one of the scenes. But like we said, Mickey doesn't just show up in the films–he's also all over the parks. These often hard-to-spot images of him are called "Hidden Mickeys" because, well, they're hidden!

But why? Think of Hidden Mickeys as a nod to Walt, the spirit of the Parks, and as a special treat for the guests. Finding Hidden Mickeys is a fun way to pass the time waiting in the decorated queues. In this exciting chapter, we reveal dozens of Hidden Mickeys in the Parks and Downtown Disney!

Disneyland

1. Adventureland - On the Jungle Cruise, check out a cast iron pan with a familiar shape inside of it.
2. Adventureland - Tarzan's Treehouse has a very cool Hidden Mickey made of rope. Look for it holding up a curtain.
3. Adventureland - The Adventureland Bazaar is home to a Hidden Mickey. Look for a Mickey head on a wall inside of a wooden circle.
4. Adventureland - The Indiana Jones Adventure has a Mickey hidden in its hieroglyphs on the well. This one is hard to spot!

5. Critter Country - While waiting in line for Splash Mountain, look in the barn to see crank gears in the shape of a Mickey head.
6. Critter Country - One of the tree knots on Splash Mountain's warning sign has a Hidden Mickey. This one is a bit hard to find!
7. Critter Country - The Briar Patch Gift Shop has a Mickey-shaped lettuce head on a shelf.
8. Critter Country - In the Many Adventures of Winnie the Pooh ride, look for a Mickey hat near Pooh's honey bottles as he falls asleep in his room.

9. Fantasyland - The Village Haus restaurant has a Hidden Mickey painted in gold on the back of a model ship.
10. Fantasyland - On the Alice in Wonderland ride, keep your eyes open for a hidden Mickey in red pain splashed on one of the Queen's hedges.
11. Fantasyland - While climbing aboard a Storybook Land Canal Boat, look for Hidden Mickeys painted on the floral designs.
12. Fantasyland - When starting the wait for Peter Pan's Flight, look up to a window with toys. A Hidden Mickey is located in the teddy bear's paw.
13. Fantasyland - On King Arthur's Carousel, a horse named Jingles has three jewels in the shape of a Mickey head.
14. Fantasyland - When waiting in line for to meet Tinker Bell in Pixie Hollow, looking for the "Fairies Welcome" sign. On the post, you'll see a Mickey head carving.

15. Fantasyland - Mr. Toad's Wild Ride has a Hidden Mickey in the corner of the stained glass window. You'll see this door right after the suit of armor falls.
16. Fantasyland - Look for a wooden Mickey head at the top of the pirate ship in Pinocchio's Daring Journey toward the end of the ride.

17. Frontierland - The Golden Horseshoe stage has a Hidden Mickey in one of the vents at the bottom of the stage.
18. Frontierland - At the top of the Mark Twain Riverboat, look for a Mickey head in the iron bars next to the smokestacks.
19. Frontierland - In the Rancho del Zocalo Restaurante, look for a Hidden Mickey near the condiments.
20. Frontierland - On Big Thunder Mountain, look for three large gears that are shaped like a Mickey head.

21. Main Street, U.S.A. - In City Hall, look for a painting with Mickey Mouse holding a child's hand. On the other side is a man in a white t-shirt. On the back of his shirt is a Hidden Mickey.
22. Main Street, U.S.A. - In the Main Street Magic Shop, a Hidden Mickey is made out of white trick rope in a display case.
23. Main Street, U.S.A. - If you wander the corners of Main Street, you'll see the Disneyland Casting Agency. The sign for the agency has two Hidden Mickeys at the top and one at the bottom, made of gold leaf.
24. Main Street, U.S.A. - The Market House has an iron decoration with Mickeys around the rim.

25. New Orleans Square - The famous Blue Bayou restaurant has stained glass in its lobby. Look to the top and spot three circles of glass in the shape of a Mickey head.
26. New Orleans Square - During the Haunted Mansion, look for the ballroom scene with the ghosts. On a table, there are three plates together in the shape of Mickey's head.
27. New Orleans Square - Pirates of the Caribbean has a difficult-to-spot Hidden Mickey in the final area. As the pirates fire shots at one another, look to the left for a gold armor hanging on the walls behind the barrels of explosives. In the center of the gold armor chest plate is a Hidden Mickey.

28. New Orleans Square - When you first splash down in Pirate of the Caribbean, look for a beach with crabs. You'll spot three shells in the sand in the shape of a Mickey head.

29. Toontown - The Fireworks Factory has a pink firework coming out of the red brick. Look for a blue Hidden Mickey painted on it.
30. Toontown - Mickey's House has a Hidden Mickey in the projector screen. The countdown circle has two black ears.
31. Toontown - In Minnie's House, look for a Hidden Mickey on a book between *Little Mouse of the Prairie* and *Cheese and Remembrance*.
32. Toontown - The lamp between Mickey's House and Chip 'n' Dale Treehouse has Hidden Mickeys.

33. Tomorrowland - Little Green Men Store Command, when you exit Buzz Lightyear's Astro Blasters, has a Hidden Mickey surrounded by rings at the top of the displays.
34. Tomorrowland - The speakers for Space Mountain on the seats are in the shape of a Hidden Mickey.
35. Tomorrowland - When in line for Star Tours - The Adventures Continue, look for a Hidden Mickey on C-3PO's top display monitor.
36. Tomorrowland - Buzz Lightyear's Astro Blasters has a hidden Mickey on the Scrabble-like wooden blocks in the first room.

Disney California Adventure

37. Buena Vista Street - The Five & Dime Band's car has Hidden Mickeys on the tire rubber.
38. Buena Vista Street - The black alarm bell in Oswald's Filling Station is has Mickey ears.
39. Buena Vista Street - Elias & Company's men's department has iron bars in the shape of Mickey heads.
40. Buena Vista Street - Julius Katz & Sons display window has Mickey-shaped watch parts.

41. a bug's land - The beverage stand that serves Fanta has cherries in the shape of a Mickey head.
42. a bug's land - Flik's Flyers have a Hidden Mickey in the concrete where the circular metal plates line together.
43. a bug's land - It's Tough to be a Bug! has three mushrooms that line up to look like a Mickey head. They are located to the left of the stage and a bit hard to find.
44. a bug's land - At the end of Heimlich's Chew Chew Train, look for a rock wall with three stones that appear to be a Hidden Mickey.

45. Cars Land - In the line for Radiator Springs Racers, look for three circular cactus in the shape of Mickey's head.
46. Cars Land - The Radiator Springs Racers have a Hidden Mickey in the projections on the walls when the tractors tip.
47. Cars Land - Look for a Mickey in the paint on the red tool shed with wheels right after Guido's Casa Della Tires.
48. Cars Land - Mater's Junkyard Jamboree has a Hidden Mickey made of hubcaps in the top corner of the queue.

49. Grizzly Peak - During Soarin' Around the World, look for three hot air balloons to make a Hidden Mickey.

50. Hollywood Land - Outside of the Animation Building, look for a Mickey Head at the top of the flagpole.
51. Hollywood Land - If you're looking for an easy-to-spot Mickey, go into the Sorcerer's Workshop in the Animation Building. There, you'll spot Mickey-shaped balloons at the drawing station.
52. Hollywood Land - In the line for Monsters Inc. Mike & Sulley to the Rescue! look for the yellow cabs in the artwork on the televisions that have upside down Hidden Mickeys near the grill.
53. Hollywood Land - The Monsters Inc. ride also has a furry Sulley animatronic where he has a purple spot in the shape of Mickey's head on his bottom.

54. Paradise Pier - The Little Mermaid ~ Ariel's Undersea Adventure has a Hidden Mickey in the shape of barnacles on the mural when loading into the clam shells.
55. Paradise Pier - The pole of the Jumpin' Jellyfish has a Hidden Mickey painted on it.

56. Paradise Pier - Goofy's Sky School has a Hidden Mickey on the wrench toward the exit.
57. Paradise Pier - Toy Story Midway Mania has Jessie and friends in three circles that make up a Hidden Mickey. Spot this when you're loading for the ride.

Downtown Disney

58. D Street - The brick wall covered in art is in the shape of a Hidden Mickey.
59. Something Silver - There is a mosaic swirl that is easy to spot.
60. World of Disney - This store is almost a literal gold mine of Hidden Mickeys. Scan the murals to the statues to the railings for Hidden Mickey. To start, look for the blue Mickey head at the top of the World of Disney sign.

CHAPTER TWENTY-ONE

DISNEYLAND MYTHS AND LEGENDS

Introduction

Over the past 60 years, The Disneyland Resort has garnered its share of legends and myths. Some speak of cats roaming the grounds at night while others worry about ghosts that come out after dark. Could any of these legends be true?

You might be surprised to know that many of these myths are heavily based in reality. In fact, some of the craziest myths of them all could be completely real! While many of the rumors might just be material of the imagination, we'll pick them apart and tell you the fact. This section contains a list of some of the most popular myths surrounding the Disneyland Park.

Disneyland Park Legends

Haunted Mansion Death Certificate

The Legend: At the end of the Haunted Mansion ride, ask for a "death certificate". These are given out only rarely and to certain guests.

Reality: Fiction.

Notes: Contrary to what many believe, there never has been a "death certificate" and any you find on the internet are not authentic. Some say that this certificate is only passed out from time to time, but all copies found have been a hoax. Maybe, one day, Disney will honor this!

Jungle Cruise Maps

The Legend: At the end of the Jungle Cruse ride you can ask for a free map.

Reality: Fact!

Notes: Unlike the "death certificate", this one was real! After unloading from the Jungle Cruise boat, you once could ask a Cast Member for a free map. These, however, are a bit difficult to get. If you're crazing a free map of the Jungle Cruise river, head to the ride at the start of the day. As soon as you leave the ride, ask a cast member at the exit for a map. Many times, they run out of these in the early morning.

Pirates of the Caribbean Skull

The Legend: In the ride, on the headboard of the treasures room is a real skull and bones. Some of these bones were taken from the UCLA Medical Center.

Reality: Likely Fiction.

Notes: While it's crazy to think that a real person's bones could be buried inside of the ride, it appears that this is a work of fiction. We believe if there is any fact in it, the bones may have been cast from actual ones, but they are not real. However, Disneyland hasn't confirmed this, so we may never truly know!

Disneyland Birth

The Legend: If a child is born in the park, he or she will get a lifetime membership to Disneyland.

Reality: Fiction.

Notes: In 1979, a baby girl was accidently born at Disneyland (the first person ever born at the park). However, it remains just a myth that she was ever given a free lifetime membership to the park. She did, however, get her photo taken with Mickey and his friends! Expectant mothers are advised to induce labor elsewhere.

Fact: Since its opening, 4 babies have been born at the Disneyland Resort. All of them have been girls!

Club 33: Disneyland's Private Club

The Legend: There is a very exclusive club in Disneyland with gourmet chefs and alcohol.

Reality: Fact!

Notes: Club 33 is very real and you can see the door to the right of the Blue Bayou in New Orleans Square (though the entrance is a bit further down). However, it is very exclusive and you have to be invited to dine or drink there. If you know someone with a membership, they can allow you inside by reserving you on the guest list. The initiation fee is $25,000 plus dues of $10,000/year and the waiting list is *years* long. Club 33 members get loads of benefits from free park tickets to sneak peaks.

For more information, visit: **www.disneylandclub33.com** (not an official website).

The Matterhorn Basketball Court

The Legend: Inside of the Matterhorn is a half basketball court.

Reality: Fact!

Notes: Designed for the climbers of the Matterhorn in their spare time, the basketball court is a small stress reliever. Unfortunately, this is not open to guests.

Disneyland Dream Suite

The Legend: There is a magical, princess-themed suite in the Disneyland Resort that allows guests to stay overnight inside of the park!

Reality: Fact!

Notes: During certain contest times, Disneyland gives away free stays in the Dream Suite above Pirates of the Caribbean.

There are signs pointing to the suite located in New Orleans Square.

Tomorrowland Edible Plants

The Legend: All of the plants are edible.

Reality: Fact!

Notes: Look for beautiful cabbages, herbs, cornstalks, and fruit trees all over Tomorrowland. The area's theme is a "space colony", hence why the plants might need to be edible in the future. While not every part of these plants are edible, they could be trees that bear fruit. Disneyland doesn't recommend that you eat these plants, so please admire them without touching.

Disneyland Cats

The Legend: Disneyland is home to dozens of cats that roam the grounds at night.

Reality: Fact!

Notes: Cats indeed run about the park and sometimes you can see them wandering at night! The cats are well-fed and encouraged to stay there to keep down the population of rats that might otherwise infiltrate the park. During the day, the cats go behind the scenes to rest up before starting their late-night prowling.

"Andy's Coming!"

The Legend: If you yell "Andy's coming!" to the costumed characters of Pixar's *Toy Story*, they will all instantly drop and freeze.

Reality: No longer Fact

Notes: Video on the internet suggests that this was once true, however, they don't do this anymore. It's not recommended to yell "Andy's Coming" at the characters as it won't work.

Walt's Apartment

The Legend: Walt Disney kept a private apartment in the Disneyland Park.

Reality: Fact!

Notes: You can see it on Main Street, U.S.A., just above the firehouse. Backstage tours will often guide inside of this space that is now a small museum dedicated to the visionary.

To book a tour, call (714) 781-8687.

Tattoos are Banned from Disneyland

The Legend: Guests must cover up all tattoos before entering the park.

Reality: Fiction

Notes: Though magazines have published that Disneyland bans tattoos, this is completely false. In fact, you'll see many, many guests with tattoos from head to toe - many of them Disney related! The only rule is that tattoos that are offensive or contain nudity must be concealed.

Walt Disney is Frozen

The Legend: Walt Disney is cryogenically frozen at the Disneyland Park and will be reanimated in the future when he can be cured.

Reality: Fiction

Notes: Walt Disney was a private man, so the public wasn't privy to the details surrounding his death. However, Walt's grave is located in Glendale California right across from the studio where many of Disney's most famous movies have been filmed or animated. His body is also buried in Glendale at the Forest Lawn Memorial Park (where Michael Jackson was buried as well).

$1 Tickets

The Legend: When Disneyland first opened, an adult ticket was just $1.

Reality: Fact!

Notes: It's true that when the Disneyland Park first opened in 1955, admission for an adult was only a buck! Even crazier was that kids were just 50 cents each. Now, you might argue that with inflation that's not a big variance. However, it's not! $1 in 1955 works out to about $8.85 in 2018. Considering that an average Disneyland ticket is over $100, that's a huge pricing difference (also keep in mind that there are many more attractions these days).

$1 Tickets

The Legend: When Disneyland first opened, an adult ticket was just $1.

Reality: Fact!

Notes: It's true that when the Disneyland Park first opened in 1955, admission for an adult was only a buck! Even crazier was that kids were just 50 cents each. Now, you might argue that with inflation that's not a big variance. However, it's not! $1 in 1955 works out to $8.85 in 2017. Considering that an average Disneyland ticket is over $100, that's a huge pricing difference (also keep in mind that there are many more attractions these days).

Disneyland Ghosts

The Legend: Close to a dozen ghosts haunt the grounds of Disneyland after the guests have gone home.

Reality: Unconfirmed

Notes: It depends what you believe, but many Cast Members have reported seeing strange apparitions late at night after the guests have gone. Disneyland attempts to keep these ghost stories alive to entertain guest. For instance, they posted a video on YouTube showing a Cast Member in the former Twilight Zone™ Tower of Terror ride and a ghostly figure flicking in an empty seat. However, it was later discovered to be a thing of Disney magic. Someone also supposedly died of fright when Disney first opened The Haunted Mansion in the 1960's. So the designers had to reimagine the ride to make it a lot less frightening. To this day, that deceased guest's ghost is said to live within the walls of the attraction.

CHAPTER TWENTY-TWO

UNIVERSAL STUDIOS HOLLYWOOD, LA, AND SAN DIEGO

Introduction

If you're planning an extended stay at the Disneyland Resort, we'd highly recommend getting out and experiencing other attractions in Southern California. Both Los Angeles and San Diego are filled with world-class sights and amusements to make your trip even more magical!

The Disneyland Resort is about 35 miles from Hollywood and 95 miles from San Diego. That means that they are so close that you could leave in the morning and return the same day to Disneyland! Here, we've outlined tips and travel advice for visiting Universal Studios Hollywood, attractions in LA, and San Diego highlights.

Universal Studios Hollywood

The world famous Universal Studios Hollywood is dubbed "the entertainment capital of the world" for some very good reasons! With thrilling rides based on famous films like "Harry Potter" and "Jurassic Park", this amusement park studio is the real deal! The tram tour is a 50-minute ride into actual Hollywood filming sets and sound stages where you can see everything from props to famous landmarks (like Wisteria Lane from *Desperate Housewives* and the house from Alfred Hitchcock's *Psycho*). Not only will you see *how* Hollywood magic is made, but you'll also *experience* it, firsthand, as you enter the Wizarding World of Harry Potter and the ancient cursed tomb of The Mummy! Universal Studios makes an extremely fun and worth-while addition to your Disneyland trip!

Getting There

By Car – From the Disneyland Resort, we recommend traveling by car. Whether you are driving your own car or renting one, traveling there is easy.

Directions:

1. I-5 North Freeway to 101 Hollywood Freeway
2. Exit Universal Studios Blvd
3. Follow the signs to Universal Studios Hollywood

Parking - Universal Studios charges $20 for General Parking in one of their garages. You can also select to preferred parking for $30, which will get you closer to the resort. However, if you are looking for extra close parking, we would recommend Front Gate Parking instead for $40. You'll be much closer to the park than with preferred. However, if you don't mind walking a bit through Universal mall, CityWalk, we recommend saving the money and getting General.

Tips Before You Go

1. **Enough for a Day** – Universal Studios Hollywood is a much smaller area than the Disneyland Resort and it's split into two levels – the upper lot and the lower lot. However, the lower lot only has 3 rides (a water-themed Jurassic Park ride, a 3-D Transformers ride, and a Revenge of the Mummy indoor rollercoaster). The upper level has the entire Hogsmeade Village from Harry Potter (which includes 2 rides, Harry Potter and the Forbidden Journey and a family-friendly rollercoaster), The Simpsons ride, and a Despicable Me ride. The real bulk of the attractions are located in the World-Famous Studio Tour tram which guides you around the backlots of Universal Studios as well as simulation rides like Fast and Furious Supercharged and King Kong 360. There are also a handful of shows and a creepy, zombie-filled haunted house themed after The Walking Dead. With that said, you'll likely get your fill of Universal in under a day.

2. **Limited Attractions for Very Young Kids** – While Disney is loaded with attractions for people of all ages, Universal mostly hits well with tweens to adults (especially those who love Harry Potter). Depending on how adventurous your young kid is (6 and under), he or she may not enjoy the experiences at Universal Studios Hollywood.

3. **Get There Early** – It's common for Universal Studios guests not to get to the park until around 11am, so getting there about 20-30 minutes before opening will allow you to experience all of the attractions early. This will also help you avoid waiting in long lines for the more popular rides and attractions.

4. **You Likely Won't Need the Front of Line Pass** – Front of Line is an additional cost to each ticket (between $70-150 extra per guest) and allows you to cut the line for most rides and attractions. While Front of Line does get you on the rides faster, it won't be necessary unless you are there on very crowded days (like in July or around Christmas). Like we said earlier, there is only enough to do in this park for one day, so Express Pass is better for those on a time crunch.

5. **Halloween Horror Nights is Amazing!** – If you're visiting in September or October, you may be able to experience one of coolest Halloween theme parks ever! Universal Studios Hollywood transforms its soundstages and backlots into terrifying thrills as lunatics with chainsaws and blood-spewing monsters chase you down Hollywood sets! You'll also experience horrific terrors in twisted mazes themed after movies like *The Shining* and TV series like *American Horror Story*. The Hollywood actors and special gore effects really make this one terrifying and fun experience! Needless to say, we don't recommend this experience for the kids! Horror film-loving teens and adult, however, find it awesome!

6. **Many Motion Simulation Rides** – Since Universal Studios Hollywood takes aim at pulling its visitors into the movies, many of its attractions are based around motion simulation. This means the ride chair or vehicle moves along with a screen to simulate you driving, flying, crashing, and escaping action sequences (think Star Tours). In fact, of Universal's nine rides, five of them use motion simulation, including its Studio Tour tram. So, if attractions like this make you feel ill, you may want to consider this before heading to Universal Studios.

★ **Magic Tips** ★

The earlier you buy your Halloween Horror Nights ticket, the better. Weekends tend to sell out, especially in October. Be sure to get to Horror Nights early to avoid the crazy lines (near Halloween, the lines can be 5 hours long!). Also, Horror Nights is the one time that Front of Line makes the most sense. You'll likely pay about $100-$150 more for it, but it will ensure that you experience ever maze and chill that evening.

For tickets: **http://www.halloweenhorrornights.com**

7. **Buy Your Ticket Early** – Save money on your Universal Studios Hollywood ticket by purchasing before you go from their website: www.universalstudioshollywood.com. However, Universal Studios does sell tickets at the gate. Online, adult ticket prices range from $105-$116 ($99-$110 child), depending on the day. Weekends and holidays tend to be more expensive. Buying at the gate will cost an additional $20 per ticket.

★ **Magic Tips** ★

Discount tickets are often sold through AAA, military bases and nearby college campuses, Costco (annual pass), and travel websites like Expedia. We usually see a $5-$10 per ticket difference in cost from the website.

The Wizarding World of Harry Potter

Experience the magic of Harry Potter come to life at Universal Studios Hollywood! Step right into Hogsmeade Village as a Muggle and leave a Wizard! Buy a school robe and wand at Ollivanders and cast spells that interact with the area. See magical creatures, escape a dragon, sip Butterbeer, and even ride a Hippogriff in this unique and fascinating world!

Rides

World Famous Studio Tram

Description: Hop aboard a large tram and visit actual Hollywood sets! The tram also gets attacked by Jaws, King Kong, gangsters from Fast & Furious and faces the wrath of many elements including massive earthquakes and flood!

Level: Everyone

Location: Upper Lot

Recommendation: An unforgettable 50-minute ride for everyone.

Note: *Fast & Furious - Supercharged and King Kong 360 are all part of this tram tour.*

⋆ **Magic Tip** ⋆

To better spot celebrities and live tapings, plan your tram tour on a weekday and in the late morning before lunchtime.

Harry Potter and the Forbidden Journey

Description: Walk through Hogwarts Castle to meet Harry, Hermione, and Ron before boarding a 3-D motion simulation ride like nothing you've ever experienced! The queue for this ride is an amazing journey through Hogwarts castle!

Level: Kids, Teens, Adults, Thrill Riders

Location: The Wizarding World of Harry Potter, Upper Lot

Recommendation: Easily the most amazing ride in the park! Harry Potter fans 7 and up will love this unique thrill ride. It does, however, get a bit spooky, but is a smile-inducing spectacular!

Flight of the Hippogriff

Description: A family-friendly outdoor roller coaster designed after a flying hippogriff from Harry Potter.

Level: Families

Location: The Wizarding World of Harry Potter, Upper Lot

Recommendation: A short and fun coaster for families with kids. The seats to this ride are very small so taller and larger adults may not find them comfortable.

The Simpsons Ride

Description: The world's favorite cartoon family brings their crazy antics to this hilarious motion simulation ride.

Level: Tweens, Teens, Adults, Thrill Riders

Location: Upper Lot

Recommendation: The humor might be a little crude for young kids, or it may go over their heads entirely. But The Simpsons ride is a hilarious adventure that we highly recommend.

The Walking Dead Attraction

Description: Step into a bone-chilling abandoned and zombie-filled building. Live actors and animatronics bring this terrifying haunted house to life!

Level: Thrill Riders

Location: Upper Lot

Recommendation: Only for those who love a good scare! This one is super creepy!

Jurassic Park - The Ride

Description: Start by floating down a gentle river and spot giant animatronic dinosaurs all before the raptors attack and you fall down an 80-foot plunge!

Level: Thrill Riders

Location: Lower Lot

Recommendation: If you like Splash Mountain, you'll love Jurassic Park. Only second in fun to Harry Potter and the Forbidden Journey, Jurassic Park is not to be missed!

★ **Magic Tip** ★

If a child in your party doesn't want to ride, enter the child swap line in the queue. One adult will wait for the child and switch when the boat finishes. Look for signs before you enter the queue.

Transformers: The Ride-3D

Description: Help the Autobots keep the Allspark away from the deadly Decepticons in this explosive 3-D motion simulation ride.

Level: Kids, Teens, Adults, Thrill Riders

Location: Lower Lot

Recommendation: A heart-pumping ride perfect for most.

Revenge of the Mummy

Description: An indoor rollercoaster themed after The Mummy.

Level: Thrill Riders

Location: Lower Lot

Recommendation: A high-speed roller coaster than lags a bit at the end, but has some pretty cool special effects. Thrill riders will appreciate this indoor coaster.

Despicable Me Minion Mayhem

Description: Ride with Gru, his kids, and of course, dozens of yellow minions in this 3-D motion simulator.

Level: Families

Location: Upper Lot

Recommendation: Perfect for families and fans of Despicable Me, but thrill riders might be okay with skipping this one.

Silly Swirly Fun Ride

Description: A Dumbo-like ride themed after Despicable Me

Level: Young Kids, Kids

Location: Upper Lot

Recommendation: A rotating ride perfect for young kids.

Super Silly Fun Land

Description: A water soak zone playground

Level: Young Kids, Kids

Location: Upper Lot

Recommendation: A mini-water park intended for young kids. Be sure to bring a change of clothes!

Shows

WaterWorld (Upper Lot) - An explosive stunt show on the water starring characters and themes from the film *Waterworld*. The explosions and stunts are fantastic and really like nothing you'll see anywhere else.

⋆ **Magic Tip** ⋆

The closer you sit to the water, the better chances you have of getting wet. To stay dry, keep out of the labeled soak zones.

Ollivanders (Wizarding World of Harry Potter) - A short show where one lucky guest has a wand choose her or him. For hardcore Harry Potter fans, this is a must. However, others may not find it worth the wait in line.

⋆ **Magic Tip** ⋆

There's no sure-fire way to get chosen for this attraction, but we do notice that those standing near the front and who are making good eye contact with Ollivander's assistant tend to get chosen.

Universal's Animal Actors (Upper Lot) - Trained animals like birds and dogs display amazing tricks! An adorable show for the whole family. Afterward, you might be able to take a pic with one or more of the animals.

Special Effects Show (Upper Lot) - Stuntmen show off their amazing talents in this live show. Some fun, laughs, and cool stunts (and a great way to escape the heat during the warmer months).

The Nighttime Lights at Hogwarts Castle (Seasonal at The Wizarding World of Harry Potter) - See magnificent lights and projections illuminate the Hogwarts Castle. Each of the four houses are represented by the magic of their animal from Gryffindor to Slytherin!

Dining Recommendations

Butterbeer (Wizarding World of Harry Potter) - A creamy soda or slushy with an unforgettable flavor. If you like butterscotch or cream soda, we highly recommend this. The soda version is sweeter than the slushy version, and most seem to enjoy the slushy better.

Big Pink Donut (Simpsons Area) - An enormous pink, sprinkled donut perfect for sharing. It's only about $5 and has a sweet, cake-like taste. Plus, taking a picture with an enormous Homer Simpson donut is priceless! Lard Lads sells them, but usually has a long line. To avoid this, head to the Kwik-E-Mart where they sell them usually without any line at all line.

Three Broomsticks (Wizarding World of Harry Potter) - Try some delicious British favorites in a Harry Potter-themed restaurant! We recommend the Cornish Pasties or the fish n chips!

Hog's Head Pub (Wizarding World of Harry Potter) - Adults can try a lager or a non-alcoholic pumpkin juice for the kids (it tastes like nutmeg and cinnamon!). If you like cocktails, try the delightful Pear Dazzle–a mix of vodka, lemonade, and pear cider. We've also tried mixing regular beer with butterbeer for a really sweet surprise!

Universal CityWalk - Just outside of Universal Studios Hollywood's gates is a mall filled with dining. Try fun chains like Bubba Gump Shrimp Co, the Hard Rock Hotel, and Jimmy Buffett's Margaritaville.

More Tips: Avoid the Jurassic Café. Bland and terrible burgers and sandwiches that really, in our opinion, give the Jurassic Park franchise a bad name.

Hollywood

Visit the Hollywood Walk of Fame, the famous Grauman's Chinese Theatre, and the Hollywood Highland Center where the Academy Awards are filmed. On the way, you'll see the Hollywood Sign high up on the hills. We will warn you that while Hollywood is a cool sight-seeing and photo place, it's not the fanciest. It's an authentic downtown location and the streets can feel dirty. For something posher, shop on Rodeo Drive or head to Beverly Hills nearby.

Getty Center

1200 Getty Center Dr, Los Angeles, CA 90049

See an exquisite art museum in a state-of-the-art building near Hollywood. There's even a tram that glides you to the museum! Admission is free, but parking is $15.

Even More Disney

El Capitan Theatre

Located in the heart of Hollywood, this magnificent, Disney-owned cinema hosts many of the Disney film premiers. When watching a movie here, you can often see exclusive props and promotional material before and after the screening. Also look for special events for classic Disney film screenings.
Tickets: elcapitantheatre.com

Walt Disney's Carolwood Barn

5202 Zoo Dr., Los Angeles, CA 90027

Visit the miniature barn is set to Walt Disney's love of trains and the American Midwest. See inspirations for the Disneyland Park including miniature trains and tracks. The museum is only open every third Sunday and admission is free.

San Diego Zoo and Safari Park

2920 Zoo Dr, San Diego, CA 92101
Tickets: $52 Adults (12 and up) / $42 Children (3-11)
The World Famous San Diego Zoo is an enormous landscape filled with exotic animals that the whole family will love. See everything from splashing penguins to graceful elephants on your visits. It's about a 90-minute drive (120 with traffic) and located in downtown San Diego. We recommend dining at the beautiful and delicious Albert's restaurant in the zoo.
San Diego Zoo's Safari Park is really an incomparable zoo experience. This remotely located wildlife preserve (87 miles from Disneyland) is home to even more exotic animals that roam massive fields. In fact, for an extra cost (starting at $111 per person) you can handfeed giraffes and rhinos in the Caravan Safari as you travel through the amazing enclosures during this two-hour tour. *15500 San Pasqual Valley Rd, Escondido, CA 92027*
Tickets: $52 Adults (12 and up) / $42 Children (3-11)

LEGOLAND California

15500 San Pasqual Valley Rd, Escondido, CA 92027
Tickets: Starting at $95 Adults (13 and up) / $89 Children (3-12)
Legoland is a unique park themed after the world's most famous building bricks. The park is specifically designed for families with kids. The weekdays are generally dead, even during the summer and holiday times. However, weekends can get packed with locals, but the lines rarely reach atrocious lengths. Kids ages 3-12 will love the small roller coasters, and Lego-themed attractions. Parents will love the short lines. Teenagers and solo adults will find that Legoland is missing experiences designed for them. However, the park is clean, well-kept and fun for families.
Discount tickets are available through CITYPass, Costco and AAA.

CHAPTER TWENTY-THREE

PRE-PLANNED RIDE AND ATTRACTION LISTS

Introduction

Want to avoid long lines and enjoy your day more? These pre-planned guides proven to just do that! Whether you are there for days on end or trying to get to both parks in one day, we have you covered. Review these lists and have fun!

★ **Magic Tips** ★

1. Get to the park early and grab a map at the entrance.
2. Take a photo of ride list you've chosen with your phone or cut it out to take with you.
3. Make all of your lunch and dinner before arrival.
4. Take a break when you need to in between rides.
5. Keep calm, enjoy the sights, and take in the magical feelings of The Happiest Place on Earth!

Note: *Your FastPass may not sync with our suggested time. You may have to switch a ride placement if this happens.*

Disneyland

Thrill Riders

1. **Space Mountain FastPass** (Tomorrowland)
   The FastPass distribution is located to the right of the ride's queue. You won't ride Space Mountain just yet.
2. **Star Tours** (Tomorrowland)
3. **Buzz Lightyear Astro Blasters** (Tomorrowland)
4. **Matterhorn Bobsleds** (Fantasyland)
   Ask to the Cast Member if you can ride the left side rollercoaster (Tomorrowland side) for the faster speeds.
5. **Mad Tea Party** (Fantasyland)
6. **Sleeping Beauty Castle Walkthrough** (Fantasyland)
7. **Space Mountain** (Tomorrowland)
   use your FastPass
8. **Star Wars Launch Bay** (Tomorrowland)
   Meet the cuddly Chewbacca or the scary Kylo Ren
9. **Indiana Jones Adventure FastPass** (Adventureland)
10. **Jungle Cruise** (Adventureland)
11. **Splash Mountain** (Critter Country)
12. **The Haunted Mansion** (New Orleans Square)
13. **Big Thunder Mountain Railroad** (Frontierland)
14. **Pirates of the Caribbean** (Adventureland)
15. **Indiana Jones Adventure** (Adventureland)
    use your FastPass
16. **Disneyland Fireworks** (Main Street, U.S.A.)

Still have more time? Ride your favorites again, hop on board a Disneyland classic like Peter Pan's Flight, or watch the Disneyland Fireworks show!

Classic Disneyland

1. **Space Mountain FastPass** (Tomorrowland)
   The FastPass distribution is located to the right of the ride's queue. You won't ride Space Mountain just yet.
2. **Star Tours** (Tomorrowland)
3. **Finding Nemo Submarine Voyage** (Tomorrowland)
4. **Matterhorn Bobsleds** (Tomorrowland)
5. **Peter Pan's Flight** (Fantasyland)
6. **Mad Tea Party** (Fantasyland)
7. **"it's a small world"** (Fantasyland)
8. **Mickey or Minnie's House** (Mickey's Toontown)
9. **Space Mountain** (Tomorrowland)
   use your FastPass
10. **Indiana Jones Adventure FastPass** (Adventureland)
11. **Jungle Cruise** (Adventureland)
12. **Pirates of the Caribbean** (New Orleans Square)
13. **The Haunted Mansion** (New Orleans Square)
14. **Indiana Jones Adventure** (Adventureland)
15. *use your FastPass*
16. **Big Thunder Mountain Railroad** (Frontierland)
17. **Disneyland Fireworks** (Main Street, U.S.A.)

Still have more time? Ride your favorites again, hop on board a Disneyland classic like Peter Pan's Flight, or watch the Disneyland Fireworks show!

With Young Kids (Ages 2-5)

1. ***Peter Pan's Flight** (Fantasyland)
2. ***Dumbo the Flying Elephant** (Fantasyland)
3. **Storybook Land Canal Boats** (Fantasyland)
4. **Fantasy Faire** (Fantasyland)
   Meet a princess and/or see a short theatre show
5. ***Mickey's Soundsational Parade** (Main Street)
6. ***Alice in Wonderland** (Fantasyland)
7. ***"it's a small world"** (Fantasyland)
8. ***Finding Nemo Submarine Voyage** (Tomorrowland)
9. **Tarzan's Treehouse™** (Adventureland)
10. ***The Many Adventures of Winnie the Pooh** (Critter Country)
11. **Disneyland Fireworks** (Main Street, U.S.A.)

**Attractions we recommend the most for preschoolers.*
*We understand that a list like this may not be so cut and dry when it comes to dealing with a fickle preschool-aged child. We recommend spreading out each attraction, and if you're met with resistance, venture into a gift shop, grab a snack, or enjoy the sights of Disneyland - or head back to the hotel for a nap. Even if you only get the attractions with a * next to it, you've had a successful and memorable day!*

With Kids (Ages 6-10)

1. **Peter Pan's Flight** (Fantasyland)
2. **Dumbo the Flying Elephant** (Fantasyland)
3. **Gadget's Go-Coaster** (Mickey's Toontown)
4. **Roger Rabbit's Car Toon Spin** (Toontown)
5. **Mickey or Minnie's House** (Toontown)
6. **Mad Tea Party** (Fantasyland)
7. **Alice in Wonderland** (Fantasyland)
8. **Autopia FastPass** (Tomorrowland)
9. **Finding Nemo Submarine Voyage** (Tomorrowland)
10. **Buzz Lightyear Astro Blasters** (Tomorrowland)
11. **Star Wars Launch Bay** (Tomorrowland)
    Meet the cuddly Chewbacca or the menacing Kylo Ren
12. **Autopia** (Tomorrowland)
    use your FastPass
13. **Tarzan's Treehouse™** (Adventureland)
14. **The Many Adventures of Winnie the Pooh** (Critter Country)
15. **Pirates of the Caribbean** (New Orleans Square)
16. **Paint the Night Parade** (Main Street, U.S.A.)
17. **Disneyland Fireworks** (Main Street, U.S.A.)

Note: *If your child enjoys faster rides, consider the following…*

- a. *Replace Alice in Wonderland (7) with The Matterhorn Bobsleds.*
- b. *Replace Autopia (8 for the FastPass and 11 for the ride) with Space Mountain*

California Adventure

Thrill Riders

1. **Guardians of the Galaxy–Mission Breakout! FastPass** (Hollywood Land)
   The FastPass distribution is located near the ride
2. **World of Color FastPass** (Grizzly Peak)
   Distribution is located next to the Little Mermaid ride. The World of Color FastPass™ won't affect or be affected by other passes
3. **Radiator Springs Racers** (Cars Land)
4. **Mater's Junkyard Jamboree** (Cars Land)
5. **California Screamin'** (Paradise Pier)
6. **Guardians of the Galaxy** (Hollywood Land)
   use your FastPass
7. **Soarin' FastPass** (Grizzly Peak)
8. **Toy Story Midway Mania** (Paradise Pier)
9. **Mickey's Fun Wheel** (Paradise Pier)
10. **Silly Symphony Swings** (Paradise Pier)
11. **Goofy's Sky School** (Paradise Pier)
12. **Grizzly River Run** (Grizzly Peak)
    Skip this if you don't want to get wet.
13. **Soarin'** (Grizzly Peak)
    use your FastPass
14. **World of Color** (Paradise Pier)
    use your FastPass

Have more time? Check out Monsters Inc. Mike and Sulley to the Rescue! (Hollywood Land) or Luigi's Rollickin' Roadsters (Cars Land).

Must-See California Adventure

1. **Guardians of the Galaxy–Mission Breakout! FastPass*** (Hollywood Land)
   The FastPass distribution is located near the ride
2. **World of Color FastPass** (Grizzly Peak)
   Distribution is located next to the Little Mermaid ride. The World of Color FastPass™ won't affect or be affected by other passes
3. **Radiator Springs Racers** (Cars Land)
4. **Heimlich's Chew Chew Train** ("a bug's land")
5. ***It's Tough to be a Bug!*** ("a bug's land")
6. **California Screamin'*** (Paradise Pier)
7. **Guardians of the Galaxy** (Hollywood Land)
   use your FastPass
8. **Soarin' FastPass** (Grizzly Peak)
9. **Toy Story Midway Mania** (Paradise Pier)
10. **Mickey's Fun Wheel** (Paradise Pier)
11. **Animation Academy** (Hollywood Land)
12. **Frozen - Live at the Hyperion** (Hollywood Land)
13. **The Little Mermaid - Ariel's Undersea Adventure** (Paradise Pier)
14. **Soarin'** (Grizzly Peak)
    use your FastPass
15. **World of Color** (Paradise Pier)
    use your FastPass

**Guardians of the Galaxy - Mission: Breakout and California Screamin' are intense thrill rides not meant for everyone. If thrill rides are not your thing, you can replace these with Mater's Junkyard Jamboree (Cars Land) and Monsters Inc, Mike and Sulley to the Rescue! (Hollywood Land). Get a FastPass for Radiator Springs Racers or Toy Story instead of Guardians of the Galaxy.*

With Kids Ages 6-10

1. **Radiator Springs Racers FastPass** ("a bug's land")
   The FastPass distribution is located near "It's Tough to be a Bug!" (not in Cars Land). You won't ride the Racers just yet.
2. **World of Color FastPass** (Grizzly Peak)
   Distribution is located next to the Grizzly River Run. The World of Color FastPass won't affect or be affected by other passes.
3. ***It's Tough to be a Bug!*** ("a bug's land)
4. **The Little Mermaid – Ariel's Undersea Adventure** (Paradise Pier)
5. **Mater's Junkyard Jamboree** (Cars Land)
6. **Radiator Springs Racers** (Cars Land)
   use your FastPass
7. **Soarin' FastPass** (Grizzly Peak)
8. **Toy Story Midway Mania** (Paradise Pier)
9. **Goofy's Sky School** (Paradise Pier)
10. **Frozen - Live at the Hyperion** (Hollywood Land)
11. **Animation Academy** (Hollywood Land)
12. **Monsters Inc., Mike and Sulley to the Rescue!** (Hollywood Land)
13. **Soarin'** (Grizzly Peak)
    use your FastPass
14. **World of Color** (Paradise Pier)

Note: *If your child enjoys thrill rides, consider adding California Screamin' between Radiator Springs Racers and Toy Story Midway Mania. Be sure to check height requirements before creating this change.*

With Kids Ages 2-5

1. ***The Little Mermaid – Ariel's Undersea Adventure** (Paradise Pier)
2. ***It's Tough to be a Bug!*** ("a bug's land)
3. ***Heimlich's Chew Chew Train** ("a bug's land")
4. **Flik's Flyers** ("a bug's land")
5. ***Turtle Talk with Crush*** (Hollywood Land)
6. **Disney Junior - Live on Stage!** (Hollywood Land)
7. ***Monsters Inc., Mike and Sulley to the Rescue!** (Hollywood Land)
8. **Luigi's Rollickin' Roadsters** (Cars Land)
9. **Paint the Night Parade** (Paradise Pier)

**Attractions we recommend the most for preschoolers.*
*We understand that a list like this may not be so cut and dry when it comes to dealing with a fickle preschool-aged child. We recommend spreading out each attraction, and if you're met with resistance, venture into a gift shop, grab a snack, or enjoy the sights of Disney California Adventure - or head back to the hotel for a nap. Even if you only get the attractions with a * next to it, you've had a successful and memorable day!*

Both Parks in One Day

Note: We highly recommend purchasing MaxPass for this

Thrill Riders

Start at Disneyland and use your MaxPass

1. **Guardians of the Galaxy–Mission Breakout! FastPass** (Hollywood Land)
2. **Space Mountain FastPass** (Tomorrowland)
3. **Star Tours** (Tomorrowland)
4. **Buzz Lightyear Astro Blasters** (Tomorrowland)
5. **Matterhorn Bobsleds** (Fantasyland)
   Ask to the Cast Member if you can ride the left side rollercoaster (Tomorrowland side) for the faster speeds.
6. **Mad Tea Party** (Fantasyland)
7. **Sleeping Beauty Castle Walkthrough** (Fantasyland)
8. **Space Mountain** (Tomorrowland) *use FastPass*
9. **Guardians of the Galaxy–Mission Breakout!** (Hollywood Land) *use FastPass*
10. **Indiana Jones Adventure FastPass** (Adventureland)
    Move to California Adventure
11. **Soarin' FastPass** (Grizzly Peak)
12. **California Screamin'** (Paradise Pier)
13. **Toy Story Midway Mania** (Paradise Pier)
14. **Goofy's Sky School** (Paradise Pier)
15. **Soarin'** (Grizzly Peak) *use FastPass*
16. **Radiator Springs Racers** (Cars Land) *Single Rider Line*
17. **Splash Mountain** (Critter Country)
18. **The Haunted Mansion** (New Orleans Square)
19. **Big Thunder Mountain Railroad** (Frontierland)
20. **Pirates of the Caribbean** (New Orleans Square)
21. **Indiana Jones Adventure** (Adventureland) *use FastPass*
22. **Disneyland Fireworks** (Main Street, U.S.A.)

Must-See Attractions

Start at Disneyland

1. **Space Mountain FastPass** (Tomorrowland)
2. **Star Tours** (Tomorrowland)
3. **Matterhorn Bobsleds** (Tomorrowland)
4. **Peter Pan's Flight** (Fantasyland)
5. **Mad Tea Party** (Fantasyland)
6. **"it's a small world"** (Fantasyland)
7. **Mickey or Minnie's House** (Mickey's Toontown)
8. **Space Mountain** (Tomorrowland) *use FastPass*
9. **Indiana Jones Adventure FastPass** (Adventureland)
10. **Jungle Cruise** (Adventureland)
11. **Pirates of the Caribbean** (New Orleans Square)
12. **Splash Mountain** (Critter Country)
13. **The Haunted Mansion** (New Orleans Square)
14. **Big Thunder Mountain Railroad** (Frontierland)
15. **Indiana Jones** (Adventureland) *use FastPass*

    Move to California Adventure

16. **Soarin' FastPass** (Grizzly Peak)
17. **Animation Academy** (Hollywood Land)
18. ***It's Tough to be a Bug!*** ("a bug's land)
19. **Radiator Springs Racers** (Cars Land) *Single Rider line*
20. **The Little Mermaid – Ariel's Undersea Adventure** (Paradise Pier)
21. **California Screamin'** (Paradise Pier)
22. **Toy Story Midway Mania** (Paradise Pier)
23. **Soarin'** (Grizzly Peak) *use FastPass*

    Move back to Disneyland

24. **Disneyland Fireworks** (Main Street, U.S.A.)

With Kids Ages 6-10

Start at Disney California Adventure

1. **Radiator Springs Racers FastPass** ("a bug's land")
   The FastPass distribution is located near "It's Tough to be a Bug!" (not in Cars Land).
2. **Soarin'** (Grizzly Peak)
3. ***It's Tough to be a Bug!*** ("a bug's land)
4. **The Little Mermaid – Ariel's Undersea Adventure** (Paradise Pier)
5. **Mater's Junkyard Jamboree** (Cars Land)
6. **Toy Story Midway Mania** (Paradise Pier)
7. **Goofy's Sky School** (Paradise Pier)
8. **Radiator Springs Racers** (Cars Land) *use FastPass*
   Move to Disneyland
9. **Star Tours FastPass** (Tomorrowland)
10. **Buzz Lightyear Astro Blasters** (Tomorrowland)
11. **Peter Pan's Flight** (Fantasyland)
12. **Mr. Toad's Wild Ride** (Fantasyland)
13. **Roger Rabbit's Car Toon Spin** (Toontown)
14. **Mad Tea Party** (Fantasyland)
15. **Big Thunder Mountain** (Fantasyland)
16. **Star Tours** (Tomorrowland) *Use FastPass*
17. **Star Wars Launch Bay** (Tomorrowland)
    Meet the cuddly Chewbacca or the scary Kylo Ren
18. **Tarzan's Treehouse™** (Adventureland)
19. **Pirates of the Caribbean** (New Orleans Square)
20. **Disneyland Fireworks** (Main Street, U.S.A.)

Note: *For faster rides, replace Mater's Junkyard Jamboreee with California Screamin' and Mr. Toad's Wild Ride with The Matterhorn Bobsleds or Indiana Jones Adventure.*

With Kids Ages 2-5

1. Start at Disneyland
2. ***Peter Pan's Flight** (Fantasyland)
3. ***Dumbo the Flying Elephant** (Fantasyland)
4. **Bibbidi Bobbidi Boutique** (Fantasyland)
   or ride the Casey Jr. Circus Train
5. **Fantasy Faire** (Fantasyland)
   Meet a princess and/or see a short theatre show
6. ***Alice in Wonderland** (Fantasyland)
7. ***"it's a small world"** (Fantasyland)
8. ***Finding Nemo Submarine Voyage** (Tomorrowland)
9. **Tarzan's Treehouse** (Adventureland)
10. ***The Little Mermaid** - Ariel's Undersea Adventure (Paradise Pier)
11. ***It's Tough to be a Bug!*** ("a bug's land)
12. ***Heimlich's Chew Chew Train** ("a bug's land")
13. ****Turtle Talk with Crush*** (Hollywood Land)
14. ***Monsters Inc., Mike and Sulley to the Rescue!** (Hollywood Land)
    Back to Disneyland
15. **Disneyland Fireworks** (Main Street, U.S.A.)

**Attractions we recommend the most for preschoolers.*
*We understand that a list (and running between both parks) may not be so cut and dry when it comes to dealing with a fickle young child. We recommend spreading out each attraction, venture into a gift shop, grab a snack, or enjoy the sights of the parks- or head back to the hotel for a nap. Even if you only get the attractions with a * next to it, you've had a successful and memorable day!*

Universal Studios

All in One Day

1. **Harry Potter and the Forbidden Journey*** (Upper Lot)
2. **Ollivanders Wand Shop** (Upper Lot)
3. **The World-Famous Studio Tour tram** (Upper Lot)
4. **Transformers the Ride*** (Lower Lot)
5. **Revenge of the Mummy*** (Lower Lot)
6. **Jurassic Park the Ride*** (Lower Lot)
7. **The Simpsons the Ride** (Upper Lot)
8. **WaterWorld** (Upper Lot)
9. **Despicable Me Minion Mayhem** (Upper Lot)
10. **Special Effects Show** (Upper Lot)
11. **Flight of the Hippogriff** (Upper Lot)
12. **The Walking Dead Attraction**** (Upper Lot)

**If this line is long for this attraction, consider the Single Rider line. You likely won't get to ride with your party, but you will get to experience the ride faster.*

***If this attraction is too scary, replace with Universal's Animal Actors (Upper Lot).*

Custom Ride List:

Names: ____________________ ____________________

____________________ ____________________

____________________ ____________________

1. ____
2. ____
3. ____
4. ____
5. ____
6. ____
7. ____
8. ____
9. ____
10. ____
11. ____
12. ____
13. ____
14. ____
15. ____
16. ____
17. ____
18. ____
19. ____
20. ____
21. ____
22. ____
23. ____
24. ____
25. ____

Custom Ride List:

Names: ____________________ ____________________

____________________ ____________________

____________________ ____________________

1. ____________________
2. ____________________
3. ____________________
4. ____________________
5. ____________________
6. ____________________
7. ____________________
8. ____________________
9. ____________________
10. ____________________
11. ____________________
12. ____________________
13. ____________________
14. ____________________
15. ____________________
16. ____________________
17. ____________________
18. ____________________
19. ____________________
20. ____________________
21. ____________________
22. ____________________
23. ____________________
24. ____________________
25. ____________________

Disneyland Resort Vacation Checklist

- ❑ Park Tickets
- ❑ Ride List
- ❑ ID
- ❑ Credit Card / Cash
- ❑ Hotel Address
- ❑ Phone (and charging cable)
- ❑ Sunscreen
- ❑ Toiletries: toothbrush, toothpaste, etc.
- ❑ Swimsuit
- ❑ Jacket
- ❑ Comfortable Shoes
- ❑ Plastic bag for cellphone (water rides)
- ❑ Snacks
- ❑ Water bottles (if you aren't flying)
- ❑ Backpack or bag
- ❑ Restaurant Reservations
- ❑ Disneyland Guidebook by Magic Guides
- ❑ ______________________________
- ❑ ______________________________
- ❑ ______________________________
- ❑ ______________________________
- ❑ ______________________________
- ❑ ______________________________
- ❑ ______________________________
- ❑ ______________________________
- ❑ ______________________________
- ❑ ______________________________

Index

D

E

F

G

H

I

J

Q

R

S

Conclusion and What's Next for Disneyland

The Disneyland Resort is always changing and so will this guide throughout the years. This is our third in the series and we want to thank you for supporting us! We sincerely hope that this book is a valuable resource for you. As noted at the beginning, we are Disneyland fans and we've created this book from our firsthand knowledge and research over many years and countless visits.

We expect a lot of changes in the next few years at the Disneyland Resort starting in 2018. Disney has already announced new lands like Star Wars: Galaxy's Edge at Disneyland and Pixar Pier at California Adventure. There will also be an Avengers rollercoaster and a Spider-Man-themed ride coming to California Adventure to accompany Guardians of the Galaxy. We also expect a name and branding change for Disney California Adventure possibly as early as 2018–our vote would be Walt Disney's Adventure Park! Disney is committed to bringing its beloved franchises to its theme parks including Star Wars, Marvel, and Pixar. So keep an eye out for more changes on the way!

Stay in the Loop!

Get Updated on Disneyland Resort changes and discounts!

Sign up for our FREE e-mail list

Visit:

www.magicguidebooks.com/signup

OR

Scan this code with your mobile device:

We believe in internet privacy and will never solicit your information.

Wishing you a magical vacation!

Magic Guidebooks

26364132R00134

Printed in Great Britain
by Amazon